THE HUMAN SOUL

ABBOT VONIER

ZACCHEUS PRESS

Bethesda

Nihil Obstat: Franciscus M. Can. Wyndham
                    Deputy Censor
Imprimatur: Edm. Can. Surmont
                    Vicar General
                    Westminster, Dec. 9, 1912

ZACCHEUS PRESS and the colophon are trademarks of Zaccheus Press. The Zaccheus Press colophon was designed by Michelle Dick.

Scripture quotations are from the Douay-Rheims translation of the Bible. The text is set in Garamond.

Library of Congress Cataloging-in-Publication Data
Vonier, Anscar, 1875-1938.
  [Human soul and its relations with other spirits]
  The human soul / Abbot Vonier.
      p. cm.
  ISBN 978-0-9830297-1-7 (alk. paper)
  1. Soul–Christianity. 2. Thomas, Aquinas, Saint, 1225?-1274.
I. Title.
  BT741.3.V66 2010
  233'.5–dc22

                                                2010040872

              10 9 8 7 6 5 4 3 2 1

To learn more about Abbot Vonier, please visit our webpage:

www.zaccheuspress.com

PATER MISERICORDIAE, EMITTE SPIRITUM TUUM UT OMNIUM HUNC
LIBRUM LEGENTIUM ET ANIMUM ILLUMINET ET COR TANGAT.
SIT RATIO ET VIA AD EXAEDIFICANDUM REGNUM TUUM.
PER CHRISTUM DOMINUM NOSTRUM. AMEN.

Contents

Introduction

"What does it profit a man if he gain the whole world and suffer the loss of his own soul?"

We understood that easily the first time we heard it, just as we understood that it applied to both male and female. In one sense, of course, no one can lose his soul; it's not like an extra ten pounds or a suntan in winter. It's pretty close to being what we are, who we are. Close, but not quite.

At death, body and soul are separated; we are human persons in the full sense when they are together. That is why it is one of the great consolations of the faith that there will be a resurrection of the body. In the end, we will be body and soul again and for all eternity. The condition of the departed before that time has been much discussed by theologians, but it remains obscure. A human soul without a body is an anomaly. *Anima mea non sum ego*, Saint Thomas Aquinas said. I am not my soul. Jesus rose into heaven, body and soul, and His Mother was assumed into heaven, body and soul. That is why we can say that she *is* His Mother, and not merely that she *was*. She could scarcely be a mother without a body and Her Motherhood has never ceased. She is a full-fledged human person right now, body and soul.

We did not need a lot of help, if any, when we first read the Sermon on the Mount. The Good News comes in on all frequencies. We have a lifetime to ponder it and as we do we turn to such authors as Abbot Vonier in order to understand it better. At first they might not seem to help. Things we had no problem with become hazy, and the lingo does not have the straightforward intelligibility of the gospels. If you were told that the verse I quoted at the outset involves the subjunctive in the if clause— as does this sentence in which I am saying so — your blank look would be pardoned. Even applauded. What difference does it make? None, really. But when an Abbot Vonier turns over in his mind the great truths of the faith and lets us in on his thinking, we are well advised to listen. At first it may put us into a subjunctive mood—would that I were reading a murder mystery—but following closely has enormous rewards.

The opposite of losing one's soul is saving it. Abbot Vonier's chief interest is to help us to save our souls.

The Fathers of the Church, when they reflected on the content of the faith, tended to ask what light philosophers might contribute. Of course they did not think that philosophy could just as such arrive at the faith, any more than they thought pure reason stood in judgment of the faith. "Beware lest you be led astray by philosophy," Paul warned the Colossians. He meant philosophers who thought they should judge the faith rather than vice versa. For all that, what philosophers had to say before the coming of Christ turned out to be helpful in understanding the faith. This is especially true in the case of the soul.

Everyone finds Plato the most delightful of philosophers, particularly when he is talking about his teacher Socrates. Back from the wars, Socrates decided to figure out what men are. You might say that he turned from the sciences to the humanities, but don't.

That makes it sound like a career move, and it went a lot deeper than that for Socrates. He wanted to live in such a way that he would be ready to die.

Plato was an artist as well as a thinker and it is not easy to tell whether what he attributes to Socrates belongs to his teacher or to himself. That is a scholarly question; meaning, uninteresting. Like who wrote Shakespeare. In the *Republic* Plato tells an unforgettable story about the human condition. Imagine a cave in which from birth men have been imprisoned, chained so as to look at the back wall. Behind them figures, statues, are held up before a fire and they cast shadows on the wall. Those shadows are real for the prisoners; they have nothing to contrast them with. So unchain them, turn them around. When their eyes become accustomed to the firelight they think that the images they now see are the real thing, not their shadows on the wall. But images are images of something, so they are led outside and see the originals of the images that cast the shadows. How unreal to them seem those shadows and images now.

Plato is talking about the liberation of the soul from ignorance. Ignorance began, he says, when the soul was put into the body. All the knowledge it had as a pure spirit is forgotten, and it must grope through life among the shadows and images and pick up intimations of the really real things it knew before birth.

Plato's view, in short, is that the soul is what we are and that our earthly condition is anomalous. Death, the release of soul from the prison of the body, restores soul to its normal condition.

Aristotle, by contrast, likened the union of soul and body to an impression in wax. You cannot lift the impression from the wax. And yet Aristotle went on to argue that the human soul is immortal; that is, survived death. What for Plato was paradise regained was for Aristotle self-hood lost. He doesn't have much to say of the condition of souls after death. Saint Thomas commends him for this. Such information as we have on the matter comes from the faith.

I suppose you could divide theologians into those who are more Platonic and those who are more Aristotelian. Abbot Vonier begins with a discussion of spiritual substance. That is what the soul is, he writes, just like God and the angels. Now that works because it is in the context of the faith that we think about the soul, and of course God and the angels are familiar to us — from the faith. Like Aristotle, though in reverse, Abbot Vonier has set a great difficulty for himself, quite deliberately, I think, and *The Human Soul* can be read as the gradual and finally triumphant overcoming of that difficulty. Abbot Vonier moves from what might seem to be an unabashedly Platonic view of soul to the Aristotelian, the process being guided by the faith. The soul as he first discusses it seems to have no more need of a body than do the angels. Everything he says in that chapter can be found in Thomas Aquinas. The difference is that Thomas would not have begun in that way. One might imagine that, after seemingly cutting himself off from it, Abbot Vonier proceeds to the great truth of the resurrection of the body.

Our lives begin in time but we are destined for eternity. Our soul is what makes us what we are. It animates the body, enables us to sense and imagine, and most importantly to think and will. Life is a drama in which we are readying ourselves to die, that is, to save our souls. The deeds we do, with the grace of God, make us what we ought to be for all eternity. It is a sobering thought that we can fail at this. That is the message of this book.

It is a learned book, but Abbot Vonier is a gifted teacher who brings the whole weight of the tradition and teaching of the Church to bear on his subject, the human soul. It is easy for us to swerve from the way and the truth and the life and become what T. S. Eliot called hollow men. Men who have forgotten their eternal destiny and try to muddle through with only those shadows on the wall. Christianity is the only adequate answer to the question, How can we be happy? Hence the Beatitudes. This book shows us where true happiness lies, and how to gain it. It is an important book, a powerful book. *Tolle et lege.* Read on.

Ralph McInerny
University of Notre Dame

The Human Soul

Chapter 1

Nature of Spiritual Substances

The human soul is a spirit. It is called the lowest of spirits by the Catholic divines. This expression ought not to convey an idea of incompleteness; it ought not to make us consider the human soul as a being that is just superior to matter without being completely spiritual substance. On the contrary, it may be asserted with perfect theological accuracy that the human soul is as much a spirit as God Himself, as much a spirit as any of the angels of God. The term "spirit" is applied with equal appropriateness to God, to the angel, and to the human soul. God, the angel, and the human soul are all alike remote from matter; they are all utterly immaterial; they differ indeed through the power of intellect, but there is no difference in their respective freedom from the laws of matter.

It is therefore my first duty to give the definition of a spirit; I must attempt to give a short theological description of the spiritual substance, at the outset, as a kind of basis to start from. To think of the human soul as of a being halfway between matter and spirit is to materialize it, is to bring it within the possibilities of heredity and evolution.

The term "spirit" primarily has a negative value, it means total freedom from the laws of space and time; it means total absence of all that is called matter, of all that is organic life; it means complete lack of sensation or sensitive life generally in the spirit-substance.

It may be safely asserted that freedom from the laws of space is the most popular and the most common condition connected with a spiritual being, even among the most primitive minds. Beings superior to himself have always been endowed by man with wonderful powers to set at naught the laws and impediments of space. It must be observed, however, that popular imagination is quite satisfied with the gift of agility, of facile locomotion, for its spirits. This, of course, popular fancy would always think to be the primary spirit-power.

The kind of freedom from the laws of space postulated by Catholic theology for a spirit is something far superior to mere agility, to mere facility of locomotion. A spirit not only moves freely within space, but he is absolutely superior to space. Space is nonexistent to him.

In fact this superiority to space, which is the most popular spirit-attribute, is one of the hardest concepts of Christian metaphysics; it requires a highly philosophical mind to find pleasure in the concept; poetry is of little avail to the philosopher when he thinks of the angelic choirs.

Freedom from the laws of time has hardly found an echo in popular imagination; all nations have made their higher beings subject to the changes of numerical time. Catholic theology on the contrary considers time to be as much against spirit-nature as space itself; it does not deny duration for spirits, but it says that the duration of a spirit-nature has nothing in common with the beat and the division of human time. Yesterday, today, and tomorrow are not divisions for the spirit. If the acts and periods of a spirit's existence are at all classified, they are classified according to more or less intensity in thought, not according to the measure of movements.

> Not so with us in the immaterial world:
> But intervals in their succession
> Are measured by the living thought alone,
> And grow or wane with its intensity.
>
> Cardinal Newman, *Dream of Gerontius*

Matter has been made as light and as bright as possible by popular imagination for a spirit-nature; but I think it would be hard to find outside Catholic theology clear and definite notions of entirely immaterial substances; even in the Catholic Church it took men a long time to rest contented with the idea of a being intensely real and yet absolutely immaterial. So late a Doctor as Saint Bernard did not dare to pronounce categorically on the subject. The lightness of spirit-substances is of course part of the popular view; it is perhaps the most cherished feature in the popular belief in angelic spirits. But Catholic theology has raised the notion of the spirit to its highest level long ago.

There is no matter in a spirit, not even matter of the most subtle kind. Even the incomprehensibly subtle ether of modern science would be like a dead weight by comparison. For a long time, in Catholic theology, spirit and matter have been oppositions, not indeed oppositions between good and evil, but incompatibilities of laws, incompatibilities in the respective modes of acting.

But freedom from matter is a small beginning, a thing which ought not to be difficult to conceive, to adhere to with mental satisfaction. We may even pride ourselves upon the ease with which we think of an entirely immaterial being, as we ourselves sigh for the day that will set us free from the fetters of our body.

Freedom from sensation, complete lack of sensitive operations, will be treated with less favor by our imagination, or even by our feelings. Both modern psychology and old Scholastic philosophy give to the sense-activities in man an exceedingly wide range. Things that are apparently of the highest order, in knowledge, and art, and sentiment, are not things of the spirit, but things of the senses, alike in the philosophy of Thomas Aquinas and in the modern researches into the activities of the brain. Activities coming under that category are as incompatible with the spirit-nature as is a heavy bodily frame; and there only shall we find the spirit where those activities give way to higher operations.

Coming now to the positive attributes of a spirit, to those perfections with which a spirit is endowed, and which would make him what he is, even were there no material Universe, I shall point out only a few for the present.

A spirit's activity is all intellect and will; his power is willpower; his size is greatness of intellect. A spirit is incorruptible, and therefore immortal, from the very principles of his nature. God might indeed annihilate a created spirit, but the annihilation would be as much a miracle as if material fire, while remaining fire, were deprived of the power of burning, through the intervention of God.

A spirit has all his knowledge inborn, or infused from above; a spirit sees everything by direct intuition. A spirit never goes back from a decision once taken. A spirit by his very nature knows all those things that are inferior to him, with the exception of the free acts of rational creatures. A spirit always acts to the full extent of his knowledge and his willpower.

These are some of the spirit-attributes constantly mentioned by Saint Thomas Aquinas; the human soul must possess them all, if the human soul is to be considered a spirit.

The objection will arise at once: "There do not seem to be in the human soul any of those great marks, either negative or positive. Our soul is alive in our body now, and yet which of us could boast of such privileges?"

To this I reply: The human soul must be considered in two totally different states, in the state of union with the body, and in the state of separation from the body. The attributes mentioned above belong to the state of separation, to the eternal, the permanent state, not to the state of transitory union. How, with the absence of those high attributes, in the present state of union with the body, our soul still preserves its perfect spirit-nature, will be our special study in one of the following chapters (Chapter 7). What I want to make clear now is this, that no spirit in its permanent, I might almost say in its normal, condition is without the qualities I have enumerated.

The doctrine that the human soul, though the lowest of spirits, is as truly a spirit as God Himself, lends itself to a few more considerations.

In the first place, it is there we are to find the reason why the human soul is truly and rightly called the image of God, is said to bear the resemblance of God, while the human body, or an animal, or a plant, or even the whole physical universe, cannot be called properly the image of God. They are the marks of God's presence, of God's omnipotence; they give evidence of His infinite wisdom; but they cannot be said, with any propriety of language, to resemble Him. The soul, on the other hand, is a strict resemblance, an exact likeness of God; this is no metaphor, it is an expression to be taken literally. And there should be little difficulty in taking the expression literally, if the word spirit applies, as we have said, with equal truth to God and to the soul. The soul shares God's immateriality and freedom from sensitive life to their full extent; these attributes (if negations may be called attributes) have the same meaning with regard to God and the human soul. We shall see, in one of the following chapters (Chapter 40), how this initial similarity between God and the soul, arising from the remoteness of each from matter, makes it possible for the soul to receive God's own Spirit, to be raised to a still higher similarity with Divinity, through supernatural grace. There is no such possibility for matter.

After stating that spirituality is possessed in equal shares by the highest and lowest spirit, the questions now arise: how then do they differ; what will be their differentiating attributes; above all, how can there be infinity of spiritual superiority for God, the Spirit of spirits, when my poor soul claims fraternity with Him?

It is the hard fate of the theological writer to be obliged to start with the most intangible points of his subject; the description of his *dramatis personae* is the most difficult part of his task, and yet the actors must be made known to the reader. The causes of differentiation between spirit and spirit, on the assumption of there being inferiority and superiority amongst them, cannot be given unless we introduce highest metaphysical principles; and yet I feel I have already spoken abstruse things, more than is wise, in this first chapter. I must be content with an explanation, which, though perfectly true, is not the last word in the matter. So let it be as follows.

Spirits differ in natural perfection through the unchangeableness and uniformity of their intellectual and volitional operations. Or, more palpably still, the higher spirit is the one to whom many objects for mind and will are as one object. An inferior spirit, when giving his attention and his love to a thousand different things, would have to do it through a thousand successive acts. A spirit of the next rank does it all through one act; and in doing it thus simultaneously, his attention to every one of the thousand things, and his love for every one of them, are greater than in the case of the spirit of the thousand distinct acts. Saint Thomas never tires of propounding this view when there is question of the various degrees of spirit-nobility, and I hold that it is as perfect an explanation of hierarchical distinction among spirits as we could desire for the present.

A theologian might pose the following difficulty to a tyro: "Which difference is the greater, the one between the soul and God, or the one between a material being and the soul?" The tyro's answer might be long in coming, as a solution of the problem cannot be obtained without making use of the rare art of sound logical distinction. On the one hand it would seem to him that a soul is nearer to God than soulless matter is to the human soul. His reason is obvious; it is because both God and the soul are spirits in the same meaning. But on the other hand there is in the tyro an innate reluctance not to make the difference between God and a creature the greatest imaginable difference.

Most likely the master himself would have to untie the knot unless his pupil were a budding theologian. The Doctor would say: "The comparison cannot be made without first making an important distinction; you will find the solution of the problem lies in the difference there is between incompatibility and superiority. The soul differs from matter because soul and matter are absolutely incompatible. They exclude each other entirely and forever. Their respective modes of being are the direct opposite of each other. Between God and the soul there is no such incompatibility in the modes of being. It could not be said that the way in which God has His perfections is in direct opposition to the way in which the soul has its own. Only with God it is an infinitely superior way of having them. Matter, on the other hand, exerts its activities in a manner that is the very contradictory of the soul's manner of acting. But the soul's attributes being those of a finite being could not be infinitely superior to matter, though they are vastly superior."

To put the thing in a nutshell: the activities of the human soul are vastly superior to those of matter, however highly organized;

at the same time their respective modes of proceeding are in direct opposition. The activities of God are infinitely superior to the activities of the soul; but their respective modes of proceeding, far from contradicting each other, follow similar lines.

Chapter 2

Spirit and Matter

The most perplexing as well as the most wonderful property of the human soul is this: the soul is found to be united with a body, with matter; how can two incompatibles be united in one person? For we have said that spirit and matter are incompatible.

Thinkers have often been perplexed by the opposition and incompatibility of matter and spirit; and their perplexity has led them to conflicting conclusions. In the eyes of many, matter is incompatible not only with spirit, but also with spirituality, with higher moral life. Matter has been condemned by some as the source of all moral evil, if not as the very substance of moral evil. "If we could but get rid of matter," they say, "we should be pure, we should be spotless in the eyes of God, we should be impeccable." Do not the saints, the ascetics, make it their life's task to rise above their material body by ignoring it and by crushing it?

Latterly, Christian Science has taken up the war-cry against matter, and its radical wickedness. But besides a war-cry, Christian Science has a strategy, a ruse worthy of the days in which Christian Science was born: it treats matter as an illusion, as a nightmare; get rid of illusion, wake up from your bad dream, and matter is nowhere. You are then all mind.

Catholic theology, although it is the most spiritual of all philosophies, has nothing in common with these premature efforts to turn man into mind, into spirit. It never found fault with matter; it never grumbled at its existence; it never looked upon it as an intruder. It loves matter as the innocent creature of God, and prays for its maintenance. Highest matter, the human body, is most dear to Catholic theology.

Opposition and incompatibility between matter and spirit is indeed the first point to be learned in our doctrine of spiritual substances. But we are warned from the very start that the opposition is not like sanctity versus wickedness, like purity versus defilement; it is a psychological opposition, and all we have to say against matter is this: Matter, even when full of life and sensation, lives and feels according to laws which, if laid on a spirit, would, *ipso facto*, destroy his spirituality. In themselves these laws are the expression of God's will and wisdom. Later on we shall see what is the real theological import of scriptural expressions like "the body of sin," "the law of sin that is in our members" (Chapter 27).

The consideration Catholic theology has for matter goes still further. In its highest state of organic perfection matter is not only good, and very good, in itself, but it helps the spiritual substance; it is, in a way, indispensable to at least one spiritual substance— the human soul.

The first principle in Scholastic psychology is this: spirit and matter are incompatible in their modes of acting.

The second principle, as important as the first, is this: the human body is raised to higher sensitive activities through a substance, the soul; and the soul, in its turn, is made perfect in will and intellect through those highly developed bodily senses.

We are not as yet asking ourselves the question, how soul and body are united in man; we assume that union for the present. We must ask ourselves a question arising from what has been said already: If there is such entire psychological opposition between matter and spirit, how do soul and body come to be united for their mutual advantage? That it is for their mutual advantage, Catholic theology holds with great tenacity. How, then, can they be of any use to each other, if body and spirit must forever follow contradictory modes in their acting?

To answer this, I shall give briefly the Scholastic doctrine of that mutual influence of soul and body which survives in the midst of their respective incompatibilities.

The soul benefits by its union with an organic, a highly sentient, body, because the sensations and perceptions of the body are for the soul, or better for the soul's intellect, the seeds of knowledge. The soul's intellect draws its knowledge from the storehouse of bodily senses. The intellect, of course, makes the sense-perceptions go much further, by means of generalizations and conclusions, than sensitive faculties ever could. But all the knowledge of the soul's intellect comes from the observation of the senses.

Now it is evident that the soul does not descend from its immateriality, does not depart from its spirit-state, by merely "taking in" the objects offered to its knowing powers by the senses. The gain to the soul is there, in spite of matter and spirit incompatibilities; it might be asserted that it is there even in virtue of that opposition, as through it the soul beholds things that are outside itself (Chapter 15).

The gain to the body from the presence of the soul is actually a more difficult problem. The soul may behold, as it were, the perceptions of the body, and make them food for intellectual abstraction; the body could never be said to receive knowledge from the soul, and thus have new sensations. Whatever happens in the soul is entirely spiritual, and therefore can never be apprehended by the body. The soul may apprehend the inferior thing, in a superior way; but the senses themselves could never reach a spiritual level. We must therefore find for the soul a way of being useful to the body which does not consist in a communication of its own activities.

A spiritual substance like the soul is, to the bodily organism in which it dwells, a principle of elevation. The spiritual principle while remaining spiritual has this power: it raises bodily senses to a higher plane by a kind of creative causality of which there are other instances in the physical universe.

This point is of too great importance not to deserve a special chapter, which I shall entitle "Elevation" (Chapter 5), in which I shall explain more fully how the bodily organism gains from being united with a purely spiritual principle.

For the present I content myself with pointing out the twofold way in which two incompatibles like matter and spirit are united for their mutual benefit. The spirit, by its presence, raises the organism to higher sensitive life. On the other hand the senses of the organism are for the mind the source of its knowledge and love. Following entirely opposite laws in their mode of acting, matter and spirit may still be helpful to each other, may still be wedded together in one personality, because of that reciprocal usefulness.

Chapter 3

Soul and Spirit

After considering the radical difference there is between matter and spirit, we have to speak of another difference, the difference between soul and spirit.

Nothing could be less in keeping with Catholic philosophy than to make the terms "soul" and "spirit" synonymous. A soul may be a spirit, and, vice versa, a spirit may be a soul. There is not between soul and spirit the impassable gulf that there is between matter and spirit.

Yet there is a vast world of souls that can never be spirits, as there is an immense world of spirits that could never be called souls, even metaphorically. It is as much against the nature of the latter to perform the functions of a soul as it would be against the nature of most souls to perform the functions of a spirit.

Generally speaking it may be said that a soul is not a spirit, and that a spirit is not a soul. The human soul is the only exception.

Speaking quite universally, spirit-functions are forever different from soul-functions. That spiritual substance which we call the human soul has both spirit-functions and soul-functions; but it is through different parts of itself that they are exercised, or rather through different powers of the spiritual substance.

Every animal has a soul; but its soul is not a spiritual substance, it is not an immortal soul; yet it is a soul, not only metaphorically speaking, but in perfect strictness of philosophical language.

By "soul," Catholic philosophy understands a principle of life and sensation for the body. The highest soul is the one that is the principle of highest sentient life. The human soul is the highest soul, not precisely because it is spirit besides being a soul, but because sentient life in the human organism reaches a height, on account of the soul's presence, which is not reached in any other animal

We shall soon come to the doctrine of our masters concerning the extent of sentient life in man. The thing in which the human soul differs from the ordinary animal soul is this: the ordinary animal soul cannot exist separate from the organism, it rises and falls with the organism, the organism that is quickened through it is also its bearer; while the human soul is capable of an existence outside the body. The death of the organism is not the death of the soul in man: it survives the organism. In that survival, however, it only fulfills spirit-functions. When the soul is united with the organism it has spirit-functions besides soul-functions; when released from the organism it has only spirit-functions; and its state is then less complete, because some of its functions are suspended.

The question might be asked: "Is the human soul more properly a spirit, or a soul? In other words, is its soul-part more important than its spirit-part?"

The answer must be, I think, that the spirit-part is predominant. It is of the family of the angels, though it may fulfill, in a higher way, the office of an animal soul. We must never forget that the human spirit has this innate capacity of being to a bodily organism the source of life and sensation.

Two definitions then are possible. We might call the human soul a soul that has spirit-functions; or we might call it a spirit that has soul-functions. The second definition is really the truer, and will be found to answer to all possible states in which the human soul might find itself. But in order of time the soul-functions precede the spirit-functions; the soul's first function is this, to be to the body the source of higher sensations, and only gradually does it rise to pure spirit-functions. Human language that speaks of the human spirit as a soul is fully justified, because in this life it is chiefly the soul-functions that force themselves upon our attention.

CHAPTER 4

Soul and God

From what has been said we ought to be prepared rather for overstating than for understating the soul's dependence on the body. Provided we safeguard the soul's spirituality and its power to have a separate existence, no dependence on the senses for its operations need alarm us.

But a connection with the body which is actually a dependence on it is for the spirit a unique position. The union between soul and body is beneficial to the soul, as we have already asserted. At the same time, it may be said that it is a source of danger to the soul, an occasion of moral loss. We feel almost instinctively that a spirit in such a position needs to be helped by God more than any other spirit.

This is why Saint Thomas is so ready to make grace a necessary element in the soul's perfection. Through grace, he says in so many words, the natural consequences of the soul's dependence on the body are corrected and counterbalanced. God is necessary to the soul in a way which is not found elsewhere on account of this dependence of the spirit on matter. God is necessary to the soul's perfection, and if God is not in the soul, the soul is morally dead. It would seem that mere union with the body, without the presence of God in the soul, would be a kind of contamination to the soul, and place it morally in a state of imperfection, in a state of deprivation.

How the soul possesses God, how God has His presence in the soul, will be the subject of another chapter (Chapter 39). What I am interested in making clear now is this, that the soul's condition requires God if the soul is to be pure and happy.

Speaking broadly, we may say that it is beneficial to the soul, from the point of view of knowledge, to be united with the body; and that there is no shadow, no drawback in such a union. It is an absolute good, it is universally true, that the soul in the body knows better than the soul outside the body.

From the point of view of moral perfection, the union could never be called an evil, because the bodily organism helps greatly in the fulfillment of moral perfection. But the union may be said to be an incomplete boon, whose very incompleteness may be an occasion of danger. Now this incompleteness is corrected or, as our masters say, healed by the grace of God, and this is why God is more necessary to the soul than to any other spirit. It may be said that He is necessary as a remedy.

This need not scandalize us; we need not ask ourselves the question: "Why does God create a being so imperfect as to be in need of His grace, if it is to be at all complete?" To this I answer that the very concept of man is the concept of a compound of spirit and matter. The soul is, after all, the lowest spirit, the next best imitation of God's perfection after the last angel. It is in the very essence of man to be in want of God; God has not made man arbitrarily imperfect, but God has made him the being that is between matter and spirit; that such a being should be in want of God is part of its nature, and therefore the position could not be considered to be something arbitrary.

There is absolutely nothing repugnant in the idea of God creating a being whose very essence postulates God's grace in order that it should be complete. The only thing we have to assume is that the grace of God is at hand whenever required.

When I speak here of the special necessity of grace for the human soul, which comes from its dependence on matter, I do not use the term "grace" in the strictly theological sense of an entirely supernatural thing. By grace I mean here additional helps given by God to the soul; what kind of helps they are, I need not discuss yet. An angel too receives supernatural grace, but an angel is not in need of any extra help to make his nature perfect, while the human soul is in need of such helps.

CHAPTER 5

Elevation, the Soul's Chief Office

The presence of the human soul in the body is essentially causative, that is to say, the soul is united with the body precisely to be for it the cause, the source, of a new reality, of a higher quality.

A union between spirit and matter which would not be causative on the part of the spirit is unthinkable. The spirit is wedded to the body as long as it is able to be to it a causative power; if matter be no longer a fit recipient of that causative influence of the spirit, the union is, ipso facto, at an end. It may be said therefore that the spirit's causative power, actually exerted on a fit material subject, is the only link that keeps the spirit tied to the body. The moment the soul's causative influence on the body ceases from lack of an appropriate subject, i.e. normally constituted organic matter, the soul turns back on itself, and enters, that very moment, upon the pure spirit-state.

This causative power of the soul on the body is, indeed, something quite peculiar. It acts as an immanent principle, not as an external agent. Its causality is called by the Schoolmen a "formal" causality, as opposed to an "efficient" causality.

A simple instance from nature will illustrate my meaning.

A tree has life and growth through two distinct sets of causes, external and internal. The external causes are numerous; sunshine and rain are the most obvious. They would be called the efficient causes, because they bring about results in the tree, though they themselves are not a part of the tree. But it is evident that there are in the plant itself causes that make it what it is, and that account for its own kind of life, its own kind of growth. These causes, whatever their nature, are called by the Schoolmen "formal causes"; they are immanent, internal; they are part of the tree's constitution. The import of the terms "form" and "formal" will be made more clear in the chapter on the "Mode of Union" (Chapter 11).

Granted, then, that the human soul has a real causative influence on the bodily organism, we must be prepared for results which are in keeping with the soul's work and energy. Our masters give to those results the generic name of "Elevation."

The soul, they say, through its causative mode of presence, elevates the bodily organism with which it is united to a higher degree of sensitive life; moreover, it elevates the higher sensitive life to the purely intellectual plane.

I must observe, however, that the second result, the raising up to the purely intellectual sphere, is not commonly called Elevation; it is the result of a power which the Schoolmen call *intellectus agens*, the causative intellect. Elevation applies more properly to the first result. Yet the principle is the same in both cases. It is a raising up in this double sense, that it leads first to higher sensitive life, and then to purely intellectual life, the ordinary animal life being the starting point.

To a mind trained in Thomistic modes of thought, man is an animal raised to the highest plane below the angelic, through an immanent principle called soul. Man is above all a rational animal, an animal that is given the non-sensitive power of reasoning, through the soul.

It would seem as if the truest view of man were this, that in him we see to what a height an animal nature can be raised by the Creator. In order to raise it to the desired height, God united to it a spirit, to be its spiritual leaven, its inherent cause of superior perfection.

The importance of this principle will justify another demonstration of the same subject. Man has organs very much like the organs of a highly developed animal. But with these organs he does immeasurably more than the animal. Thus, for instance, his brain produces results so entirely superior to those of an animal brain as to make us conclude that they are the product, not of an animal brain, but of a spirit. Yet our masters, very wisely and reservedly, consider those manifestations to be brain-manifestations, not pure spirit-manifestations; only, for them, the human brain has been leavened by the spirit; it has been elevated by a soul that is at the same time a spirit.

The Schoolmen distinguish in man three levels of phenomena. The lowest are those in which man differs in no way from the animal; the highest are those which are the results of the spirit-part of the soul: they are pure spirit-functions. Between those two classes there is a vast region of phenomena which belong to the body, are performed by a bodily organism, and yet could never be performed by a bodily organism unless that organism had been elevated or leavened by the immanent presence of a spiritual substance, the soul.

For the sake of clearness, and on account of the importance of this division, I will give instances of these various classes of phenomena. Bodily growth, sensation, emotions of anger, jealousy, sadness, belong to the first class; they are common to man and to animal.

Abstract thought, such as mathematical or metaphysical thought, free will, conscience, in the sense of its being the imperative of duty against the allurement of pleasure, belong to the third, the highest region.

What I should call the middle region is a class of phenomena that extends over much that fills the human life. Sentiment, conjugal love, the appreciation of beauty, the readiness to observe and act in the occurrences of every moment, are all matters that belong to the brain, but to the brain elevated by the presence of a spirit. The animal is not capable of them, because they are too high for it, nor could the spirit perform them, because they are not immaterial operations. Operations of that class give evidence in favor of the existence of a spiritual substance in man, because no organism could rise so high, if there were not in it a principle that is greater than matter; yet they are not the direct operations of the spirit.

We have to admit therefore in man a double series of phenomena that proclaim loudly the presence in him of an immaterial spirit. The purely intellectual phenomena are a direct proof of an intellectual or spiritual soul, because no intellectual operations could come but from a spiritual substance. It is the clearest and most direct evidence of the presence of a spirit in man. That exceedingly high sentient life in man, however, which we call the middle region of his life is urged more frequently as a proof in favor of a higher soul. How could we differ, we say, so greatly from animals if there were no higher principle in our organism? This argument is fully justified, for no difference in organisms between man and animal could account for the difference in the respective workings of their brains.

It has been the constant effort of materialists to point out the similarity between the human organism and the organism of the highly developed animals; but the greater the similarity, we retort, the greater the need for positing an elevating principle, as there would be no means otherwise of accounting for the extraordinary dissimilarity of operations in man and animal.

Chapter 6

The Catholic "Via Media" in Psychology

Catholic psychology stands or falls with the doctrine of the spirituality of the human soul. At the same time Catholic philosophy is the born antagonist of every kind of false idealism, that is to say, of systems of philosophy that do not make the bodily senses the source and means of knowledge. Normally, there are no direct communications with the spirit-world; there is no speaking under ordinary, natural, circumstances with spirits that dwell in higher intellectual spheres. All that we know, we have at one time seen with our eyes, heard with our ears, felt with our hands, or received through the other senses; except in the case of supernatural illumination.

Nihil est in intellectu quod non prius fuerit in sensu, there is nothing in the intellect which has not been previously in the senses, is the golden axiom of Scholastic philosophy. There is not one single exception to it, at least in the natural order of things. It would be an easy task to show how in everybody's case this axiom proves to be perfectly true. I may search every corner of my mind and I shall find that all my intellectual store has come to me through my bodily senses. In fact when I think myself absorbed in abstruse thoughts, I find myself using, mentally, words and images which the ear and the eye have furnished.

On the other hand Scholastic philosophy has risen to such heights of spirituality as to scandalize the materialist and to irritate him.

Evidently Catholic psychology has adopted a *via media* between rank materialism and idealism run wild. Scholasticism endows the soul with a power no other philosophy recognizes: the power of abstraction. It would not serve the purpose of this book to enter into all the technicalities of this great problem. Stated briefly, the power mentioned is this: material things contain more truths than appear to the eye; they are bearers of evidence of higher, immaterial things. Now it is the mind's office to find out the intellectual truth revealed in the material object, and it is this intellectual kernel contained in the material object that is the food of our mind. It is possible for one mind to see more intellectual truth in the material object than for another; but even the keenest mind never knew anything that was not found in a material object. In other words, our intellect deals immaterially or spiritually with bodily and material things.

To such an extent is this true, that at no stage of our mental development is it possible for the intellect to do anything without the cooperation of the senses, because the senses furnish the intellect with its proper objects. Once more, not only does the intellect handle material objects intellectually, but the intellect has nothing else to handle; and, but for their presence, the intellect could have no act of its own.

I do not say here that the intellect possesses or requires a bodily organ for its operation; it is intellect for the very reason that it has no such bodily organ; but what I say is this, that the intellect has no other objects to work upon than the objects provided by the bodily organs which in themselves are lower then the intellect.

Thus it is perfectly clear how intellectual life may be disturbed or suspended through disturbances or suspension of organic functions. The parts affected are the senses; and intellectual life has become impossible, or anyhow has been disturbed, because there are defects or disturbances in those organs that bring to the intellect its objects of contemplation.

The everyday argument of materialists against the existence of an immortal soul is chiefly this: material causes, such as anaesthetics, succeed in putting a stop to the highest intellectual life. How can there be in man a spirit superior to the body, if a small dose of gas brings his intellectual life to a standstill?

I answer that nothing warrants the conclusion of the materialist; his conclusion goes far beyond his premises. For there remains this possibility, that the mind has no other food for its operations than the impressions furnished by the senses. Nothing in the whole range of philosophy is against the reasonableness of such a possibility. Therefore it is premature to conclude from the cessation of intellectual life, through the application of anaesthetics—to quote only one of the many causes—the non-existence of a spirit in man. If sensitive impressions are the intellect's only field of action, it is obvious that, through a cessation of sensitive impressions, the mind must become inactive.

When we say that the intellect's field of action is restricted to the objects offered by the senses, we must remind the reader of a remark already made, that sensitive life, in Scholastic philosophy, has a wonderfully wide range. It goes to the extent of comparing, coordinating, and associating material objects, according to certain clear and palpable laws of causality. We presuppose all this superior work of the higher senses. If, through some cerebral infirmity, this coordination of sensitive objects cannot take place, the mind, or the intellect, lacks its normal object; it cannot reason logically. Let our brains be sound, and the intellect will take care of itself.

If once we grasp this great principle of Scholastic philosophy, that man's purely spiritual intellect depends on the organs solely because the organs have to furnish it with its congenial objects, there will be very few practical difficulties left to prevent our admitting that there is a great spirit in us, even when we feel most unfit for thought.

CHAPTER 7

The Mystery of the Soul's Unconsciousness

There is one objection against the theory that an immortal soul is part of the human personality which deserves special attention. Both the objection and the answer to it occur in various parts of this book, under different forms; yet as the matter is of unusual importance, I think it necessary to write a separate chapter on it.

I call the difficulty in question the mystery of the soul's unconsciousness. The objection may be formulated in the following way. How is it possible for a spirit to be united with a bodily organism, and yet be so entirely unconscious of its own existence, when on the other hand we find that the bodily organism has such a direct consciousness of its own acts and its own existence? For it is the verdict, not only of observation, but also of rational philosophy, and of Scholastic philosophy in particular, that there does not exist for man, here on earth, a direct consciousness of the acts and of the existence of the soul. The soul's acts are found out only through a careful process of mental sifting that reveals the presence in man of activities which are higher than the highest sensitive activities. The distinction between pure soul-acts and highest sense-acts is not immediately obvious. I do not distinguish as easily and as directly between a purely intellectual act and a purely sensitive act as I distinguish between a feeling of bodily pain and a feeling of bodily gratification. The soul's existence is a fact even more remote from consciousness: I know it only through a most elaborate process of reasoning.

But even granted that there are in man certain higher activities, which careful mental analysis will pronounce to be something totally distinct from the activities of sensitive life, there is another circumstance which adds weight to the objection. Acts of that higher order may be the manifestation of a spirit; they may tell us that in man there is a soul which is superior to the bodily organism. But how much there is of man's life that is spent without a single vestige of such higher activities! Every human individual has to spend several years without any such higher activities; the age of reason begins only when an appreciable portion of human life is already gone. Again, sleep is for all practical purposes devoid of those higher activities. Finally, there are human beings who never show any signs of the higher activities in the course of their whole life, however prolonged their existence may be; the permanently insane never show signs of rational life in the real sense of the word. It would be an easy task to multiply instances of those delays, intermittences, suspensions or even total extinctions of the higher activities in man, at the very time when a spiritual soul is supposed to be united with the body.

In fact, man's mental evolution does not seem to differ in its laws from the organic evolution in nature. It is a comparatively easy task to point out and to enumerate every one of the causes that bring about each forward step on the road of mental progress, both for the race and the individual. No Catholic theologian, with all his faith in the presence of an immortal spirit in man, would ever look for the cause of mental progress elsewhere than to external circumstances that can be classified scientifically. The soul is not the cause of progress, it is itself the thing that is made to progress. Not the internal soul, but the external world is the source of every forward movement of the human mind.

All these considerations simply bring out more forcibly the difficulty: how is it possible for a mighty substance, entirely spiritual in its nature, to be apparently so inactive, even to the extent of not being a source of mental progress? But the difficulty vanishes if we reflect on the soul's mission in the body. The soul is to the body an immanent principle of elevation; it raises the knowing and loving powers of man to a higher sensitive level than in the mere animal; moreover it raises the results of that highest sensitive life to a purely immaterial level. The soul is essentially a principle of elevation, not of progress.

It ought easily to be perceived how a spiritual substance whose whole role it is to be the intrinsic, causative principle of elevation to a bodily organism, may be intensely causative, intensely real, without having a direct consciousness of its own existence; how it may be the greatest power, the most important partner in the human composite, and yet be externally the least assertive thing. Being essentially a principle of elevation it acts to the full extent of its powers in fulfilling this function; it exhausts itself, so to speak, in elevating the human organism.

This elevation takes place in every human individual, however low he may be in the scale of mental culture; for potentially every human being is fit for both art and thought. The absence of the higher mental activities is reconcilable with the presence of a mighty spirit in man.

The spirit or soul does not cause new light, new thoughts, new views; it only elevates the results of the sensitive knowledge. The soul is not the direct cause of progress; the material world, apprehended by the senses, is the direct cause of all progress. The soul's mission is to elevate the acquisitions of the knowing powers that are in the senses to the immaterial plane and to extend them by means of logical deductions. The soul does not make new things; the soul makes higher and broader the things already existing in the sense-apprehensions.

Let the bodily organism have its normal state, let it possess its full development, so as to have highest sensitive activities, and the soul will raise the results of those activities to the immaterial plane at once, without any effort. But the body may be imperfect, may have its higher sensitive life disturbed or retarded in some way; then there is no proper, congenial matter for the soul to elevate, although the soul is always there.

The soul is neither conscious nor unconscious by itself; it is neither active nor inactive by itself; it is simply a principle of elevation to the bodily organism and to the activities of the bodily organism. It has no consciousness peculiar to itself distinct from that of the whole human compound. The consciousness, the activity, is of the body, elevated by the soul. Our next chapter will throw more light on this most interesting subject.

CHAPTER 8

The Awakening of the Soul

When our masters require a definitely human organism before the soul is united with the human body, they are under no illusion; for it is not just in order to safeguard the soul's dignity that they require a comparatively perfect organism.

The simpleminded might be ready with the following objection: "If the soul is the perfectly spiritual substance it is said to be, as soon as it comes to the body, it ought to show its presence by decidedly spiritual acts; now no such acts are possible with an un-developed organism." But it is not in order to meet reasoning of this kind that our Catholic philosophers exact a perfect organism for the union of soul and body; for, if the objection were pushed to its full logical conclusion, the adult man only could be credited with a soul.

No one ever had a higher idea of the soul's excellency than our masters; yet they all hold it as an article of Christian faith that the soul is united, and united completely and perfectly, with the body long before there is distinct conscious life. A newborn infant has an immortal soul, and baptismal grace comes to it as truly as to the adult catechumen. Therefore it is clear that the reasons which made our teachers postulate a specifically human organism before the soul is infused are to be found not so much in the soul's intellectual life as in the soul's vivifying and elevating power; a soul is united with a body to the full extent of the union as soon as the body is capable of being vivified and animated with a higher life.

Are we then to suppose that the soul is dormant for a long period of its existence in the body; that it is inactive, nay, latent, in the human organism? And if so, how are we to view the awakening of the soul, its transition from unconsciousness to the state of highest consciousness and responsibility?

First of all, not one of our masters ever held that the human soul in this life has a direct consciousness of its own existence and nature. In other words, my soul has never seen itself, has never felt itself; it is the condition of the disembodied soul alone to see and feel itself, to be directly conscious of its own nature and existence, not through laborious reasonings. It would be nothing short of a miracle if such a consciousness of the soul's nature and existence did take place in us, even for one short moment, while we live in our body. It is only through a most subtle and attentive observation of our mental life that we arrive at the conclusion that there is a soul in us, and the road to that conclusion lies high and is very toilsome. But a direct intuition of its own self is not only denied to the soul in its mortal state; such an intuition essentially constitutes the disembodied state of the soul.

Therefore, when we speak of the awakening of the soul we must not expect too much; we must not expect it to arrive at a directly spirit-like consciousness of its own self; such an awakening is the awakening of eternity, not of time.

In order to understand more clearly the kind of awakening there is in the human soul, we must again bear in mind the far-reaching principle enunciated in the preceding chapters: the soul is to the body a principle of higher life. To be such a principle is, so to speak, the whole *raison d'être* of the soul. The soul is essentially a spiritual leaven to the body, permeating the mass of the human bodily organism. The moment the soul begins that leavening it is fully active, it fulfills its mission completely. Even in the embryonic human individual the soul is indefatigably at work as the principle of a growth that soon will result in the mature human brain, with its super-sensitive powers and operations. The soul has not to awake; it is the bodily organism that has to awake; the soul's mission is to bring about that higher awakening of the brain which makes man superior to the animal. As we have said elsewhere, man is superior to the animal through his higher sensitive life, through his higher sensitive consciousness, as well as through his intellectual life. Such is the awakening of the soul; it makes the human organism awaken in due time to a life and consciousness that does not belong to the animal but is exclusively human. But as for itself, the soul always remains a hidden principle as long as it is united with the body.

The reader will remember the three regions in man's life spoken of in a former chapter. What we have said just now is the awakening of the second region, the region of highest sensitive life. What then about those soul-acts that are the third region? Are they not the soul's own workings, and therefore the direct consciousness the soul has of its own self? We say elsewhere that pure intellectual life, with its concomitant volitional life, is a direct proof of the soul's spirituality. It would seem therefore that it is also a direct revelation of the soul's existence, a direct consciousness of its own self.

Such however is not the case. My bodily activities bring home to me directly a consciousness of my body's reality. I could never doubt the existence of my body; I feel its existence through and through; I do not need long and subtle arguments to arrive at the conclusion that I have a body. But no such direct consciousness of the soul's existence is to be had, even when I am most busy intellectually. The intellectual operations are indeed the acts of the soul, but they are not acts that convey a consciousness of the soul's existence as distinct from the bodily organism; acts of that kind are reserved to the disembodied state.

To put it technically, in intellectual life the soul beholds or grasps intellectual objects, but it does not elicit what I might call spirit-deeds, deeds that reveal the spirit as clearly as sensation reveals the body.

There is an analogy of this even in our bodily faculties. I know that I have eyes because I have beheld my face so often in a looking-glass, because I have seen eyes in every one of my fellowmen; but for that I could not know that I have eyes, though my eyes are constantly beholding nature and its marvels. Eyes are all for the external visible objects of nature; if I had not a looking-glass, or if I had no fellowmen, I could still find out by reasoning that I must have organs of vision; for I perceive external objects; therefore there must be in me an organ of vision. But the eyes themselves, when they are in a normal condition, never reveal their existence directly through their activity. I do not, so to speak, feel my seeing; my eye does not see itself, though it sees everything else.

This is a mere analogy, as I have said. In the third region, the soul understands intellectual things or objects, but it does not understand itself; it must arrive at the conclusion of its own existence through elaborate reasoning.

In intellectual operations we find the highest awakening of the soul in mortal life; but even there the awakening is dependent on the perfection of the bodily organism. The objects beheld by the soul are intellectual indeed, but intellectual though they are, they are about bodily things. It is the intellectualness of material things that is the highest food of the human soul in its state of union with the body; so even our highest thoughts are intrinsically associated with material objects. Our mind cannot act intellectually without our imagination having at the same time a material and palpable image of its object.

I spoke of that psychological law in the preceding chapter, where I established that, through the very conditions of our nature, highest intellectual life is simply impossible without a vast amount of organic life that precedes, accompanies, and follows it. We should be intellectually in a state of dormancy if it were not for the awakening of our senses. Therefore—and this is the fact I want to insist upon just now—even in this third region, the awakening of the soul is merely the consequence of the awakening of the body. The soul is fully awake only when the body has reached such maturity as to be able to furnish all that higher sensitive life which has to precede, accompany, and follow highest intellectual life. Given that maturity, the soul does its intellectual work infallibly, and, one might say, of necessity.

By awakening of the soul we mean something different from the perfection of the soul. Perfection of the soul implies not only activity, but also rectitude. A soul may have highest activity and yet lack rectitude; rectitude is a different thing altogether. Many times in ordinary parlance awakening of the soul is mentioned in reference to man's moral or spiritual life, in reference to man's realization by faith that he has a soul. We speak of a soulless man, not because a man is entirely destitute of intellectual life, but because he is destitute of a practical conviction that he has a soul, or that his fellowmen have souls; intellectually he may be wide awake; yet we would call him soulless, on account of the absence of certain moral qualities. But all this comes more appropriately under the heading of the soul's perfection or rectitude, of which we treat in our next chapter.

CHAPTER 9

The Soul's Perfection or Rectitude

The soul is a spirit. Without exaggeration, one may say that spirits, and spirits only, are perfect or imperfect, in the true sense of the expression. Material things are always perfect; from the very laws of their materiality they always fulfill their aim or mission. Those beings only can truly be called imperfect that have free will. Far from making perfection the same as spirit-nature, a spirit, and a spirit only, is either perfect or imperfect, simply because he has free will. The good use of his free will makes him perfect; misuse of free will makes him imperfect.

The reader will see, therefore, that the awakening of the soul, and the moral perfection of the soul, are two very different things, following different laws; the one follows the law of intellectuality, the other follows the law of free will.

That there is such a perfectibility for the human soul is an essential doctrine in Christianity; it is, in fact, the root of Christian ethics. Perfection of the soul is the salvation of the soul; it is the eternal life of the soul. Imperfection of the soul, or more truly absence of perfection, is the loss of the soul, it is eternal death. Without this perfectibility of the human soul Christianity is incomprehensible, for Christianity is strongly psychological. Christianity is the making of the human soul; it views things and appreciates things according to the degree of perfection they give to the soul. "For what doth it profit a man if he gain the whole world, and suffer the loss of his own soul?"

I have said just now that awakening of the soul and perfection of the soul follow different laws. This does not mean that the two things have nothing in common, do not help each other. It is precisely on account of that initial dormancy of the human spirit that perfectibility is both possible and necessary. A spirit fully awake, to the extent of being directly conscious of its own existence and state, has no substantial perfectibility. The perfectibility of our soul in the moral order comes exclusively from its progressive awakening in the intellectual order; it comes from the soul's union with a constantly changing bodily organism. In the state of separation between soul and body there is no longer a real perfectibility for the human soul.

It does great credit to Scholastic philosophy that it looks for the cause of the soul's perfectibility to the changeableness and growth of the bodily organism with which the soul is united. It shows the wisdom and moderation of our masters in their theories of the spirituality of the human soul. A less wise philosophy would have made the soul's progress quite independent of the body the first condition of perfectibility. Nay, more; perfection of the bodily organism, according to the Schoolmen, makes the soul more perfect. To give one instance only: temperance and purity are essentially perfections of the bodily organism; we call them the virtues of the body. Now Saint Thomas is explicit in stating that through the bodily perfections contained in these virtues, the soul itself is made more perfect. This is why real sanctity of the soul could never be separated from purity of the body.

All the same there is one very striking thing in this matter of the perfectibility of the human soul. It is this: moral perfection may go much further than intellectual awakening in the soul. In other words, the soul's moral rectitude can be much greater than the soul's intellectual endowments. There is in the soul's moral perfection a finality that is not found in its knowledge, at least here on earth. For reasons to be given later the case is different in the next world. If knowledge is of importance here on earth it is so chiefly as an element of action, and because it leads to action, because it helps action. To such an extent is this true that perfection of the soul is possible without knowledge in at least one instance. It requires, no doubt, that supernatural influence from God called grace; but such is the state of the baptized infant.

I am of opinion that no philosopher has said the last word on the causes of the soul's perfectibility while it is united with the body, and of the cessation of that perfectibility when the separation between soul and body has taken place.

As already remarked, this doctrine of perfectibility is a part of Christian dogma, and it is moreover a part of Christian dogma that the soul is made perfect in this life more through the acts of will than through acts of the intellect.

It ought to be clearly understood that the perfection of the soul coming from the right exercise of its free will is a positive state of the soul; it makes the soul fundamentally better, just as abuse of willpower makes the soul fundamentally bad or imperfect. Repeated virtuous acts give the soul a psychological rectitude which may endure forever, unless by opposite acts this rectitude be again destroyed. All our philosophy on virtues and vices is merely the philosophy of the making and marring of the human soul. Virtue builds up the soul, vice pulls it down. The highest things in the Christian dispensation, such as the Eucharist, are a building-up of the soul; they are destined to make the soul more perfect. Catholicism knows of no redemption that is not a transformation of the human soul. Progress is the law of Catholic spirituality; it means first the repetition of virtuous acts, and then the performance of higher acts, which will result in the soul achieving a more perfect state that will endure forever.

This law of perfectibility is not an arbitrary law laid down by God; it is a necessary law which is part of the soul's essence. It would imply contradiction for the soul to be precious in the eyes of God without being intrinsically perfect. It is of course within God's power to bring about that intrinsic perfection in a supernatural way, as for instance in the case of the infant that receives baptism. But the normal way for the soul of perfecting itself is the repetition of free virtuous acts, and the striving towards nobler acts. There is no reason why we should deny to God the power of making the soul intrinsically more perfect without repeated acts; but we must consider it a contradiction that the soul should be great and yet not have its greatness in itself.

People who are intellectually inferior are often found to be vastly superior in the qualities of their will. This disproportion between intellect and will sometimes surprises us; yet it is strictly in keeping with man's present condition. It makes sanctity practically independent of the laws of scientific progress. The reason given by Saint Thomas why moral perfections in this life may go beyond intellectual endowments belongs to the region of the supernatural. By charity the Holy Spirit works on the human will directly, personally. There is no such direct or personal working on the human intellect in this life. Left to his natural powers, it does not seem that man's perfection of will could ever go beyond the perfection of his intellect.

In a later chapter more will be said concerning the body's part in bringing about the soul's perfection; but enough has been said, I think, to make it clear that the perfection of the soul is an aim worthy of man's effort.

CHAPTER 10

The Soul's Place in the Universe

The human soul holds a definite position in God's creation; it is an indispensable link in the chain of beings that constitute the universe. It fulfills a definite mission, which no other created being could fulfill. It is a note in the harmony of the world of beings; without it, there would be a dissonance.

By "universe" we mean the entire aggregate of created things, both material and spiritual. Catholic theology considers that the spirit part of the universe is its most important section, that the gradation from the lowest particle of matter up to the highest spirit is an uninterrupted ascension from perfection to perfection. There is no gap in the universe, no violent transition. The universe has never been considered otherwise by Catholic theology than as a perfect whole, in which the higher being invariably possesses all the perfection of the beings that precedes it. The universe has all the continuity of growth; even where growth is no longer possible, the theologian looks for uninterrupted continuity in the scale of beings. No men are greater believers in what might be called the interlocking of beings, than the old theologians.

Sound theology invariably starts with the question of a being's position and rank in the universe. It never begins with the exceptional, the privileged state; it leaves the exceptions to the very end. What is a being's function and mission in the universe? What is its part in the universal harmony of things? These are the first questions asked by theology. The question to ask ourselves is not exactly into what God could make the human soul, but what is required of the soul in order to make the universe one harmonious whole.

It is therefore of paramount importance for us to grasp the doctrine of our masters concerning the soul's place in the universe. According to the constant teaching of Saint Thomas, the soul's role and mission in the universe is to be the one creature that has at the same time spiritual and experimental knowledge and love of the physical universe.

The human soul must be considered as the spirit that knows and loves the material, the physical universe experimentally. Experimental knowledge stands here for knowledge received from the material, the visible and tangible objects, through the impressions made by those objects on the senses. These impressions we suppose to be true impressions, in the sense that they convey to the knowing powers the exact state of things as it is in material nature. How it is possible for the human soul, which we suppose to be a spirit, to receive true and faithful impressions from material objects, we saw in the second chapter, where it was shown how the physical world reaches the spirit through the senses, and does so without destroying its spirituality.

A pure spirit, an angel, knows and loves the physical universe; but he cannot do so experimentally, for he has not seen its beauties, heard its harmonies, or touched its material elements. The pure spirit's knowledge, according to Saint Thomas, is not the result of sensation and observation, it is directly infused by God; he is either created with such knowledge, or receives it from above in the course of his existence.

The human soul is created merely with the capacity for "taking in" the physical universe. The human soul is entirely and exclusively the spirit of the physical universe, in the sense that it is a spirit with no other knowledge, in the natural order, than the one given by the physical universe.

An animal has experience of the physical universe through sensation, but it could not be called understanding; it has merely sensations, or a combination, of sensations. The human soul has a knowledge, which on the one hand has the spiritualness of an angel, and on the other hand has the experimental character of animal sensations; but we must remember at the same time that it is neither sensation, nor angelic knowledge. And what is said here of knowledge must be understood of love too.

This view of the soul's cosmic position does not tie down the soul to the physical universe. The physical universe everywhere shows the Creator's hand. Thus the knowledge and love of the physical universe, which we say to be the soul's exclusive role, implies knowledge and love of God, as far as the physical universe reveals Him. "For the invisible things of Him from the creation of the world are clearly seen, being understood by the things that are made. His eternal power also, and divinity" (Romans 1:20).

When we say that the soul's place in the universe is to know and love as a spirit, and yet experimentally, the things of the physical world, we are far from asserting that the soul's natural end and purpose is the physical world; that is God, and God alone, manifested to the soul in the beauties of the physical universe.

It is true that the human soul has never been restricted to this merely natural role; from the very beginning God meant it to have a privileged state; from the very beginning the soul was destined for a knowledge and love higher than the knowledge and love of the physical world. It must be borne in mind, however, that the natural state is not taken away by the privileged state; it remains in its entirety, only it is no longer the last and final thing; there is now something loftier to aspire to. But over and over again we shall be obliged to bear in mind the limitations of the soul's natural role if we are to understand its powers and workings.

The soul's place in the universe may be made clearer still if we look at the matter from another point of view, namely, that of the end of the physical universe itself. It may be said that in the human soul, and in the human soul alone, there is a spiritual consciousness of the material and visible beauty and goodness of nature.

Without the human soul the physical universe must forever be barren and fruitless for the spirit-world; it could never profit in any way. It is in the very nature of the pure spirits, whom we call angels for lack of a better term, to possess all knowledge *a priori*, having received it directly from God, being created with a fullness of understanding. They do not learn from the physical universe, they do not see anything in it which they do not already possess in their intellects. It would be truer to say that the physical universe receives something from them, than to say that they learn anything from it.

Physical nature would therefore lack finality, would not be connected with the higher, the spirit part of the universe, if it were not for the human soul, for which it is the storehouse of all knowledge, the source of all love, the beginning of all greatness.

Enough has been said, I think, to make it clear that the soul's first food must be among the things that are seen with the eyes and heard with the ears, that Nature with its charm is as a mother to the human soul, and that the soul is truly the sanctuary where the world's marvels are able to praise the Lord.

CHAPTER 11

The Origin of the Human Soul

The point that is of paramount importance in the theology of the human soul is its spirituality, the fact of its being a strictly spiritual substance with operations superior to the potentialities of organic matter. The spirituality of the human soul could never be for a Christian the object of any doubt. Christianity stands and falls with the doctrine of the spirituality of the human soul. The spirituality of the human soul once established, the doctrine of the Hereafter is a direct consequence.

The spirituality of the human soul being after all the one thing that matters, it is not surprising that the origin of the soul is a doctrine which has not been as clear to the minds of Christian thinkers as has been the doctrine of the soul's spirituality. The history of this part of Catholic theology is interesting. Great names are identified with views about the origin of the human soul, which later philosophy has repudiated. Saint Augustine, for instance, was a believer in the transmission of the human soul from parent to child.

There were Doctors who thought that all human souls were created in Adam and transmitted in a state of latent existence to his innumerable offspring. We need not be surprised at these vacillations of the Christian mind about the origin of the human soul. Once granted its spirituality, the mode of origin is quite a secondary consideration.

The Church has now adopted, as a Catholic doctrine, the view that every human soul is created directly by God; but nothing would be less in keeping with the history of human thought than to imagine that this divine origin of the human soul was the starting point for the Christian mind, always prone to make God the direct origin of everything. The starting point is the spirituality of the human soul; and the doctrine of individual creation by God was arrived at simply because every other theory concerning the origin of the human soul had been found wanting. It is of great importance to bear in mind this secondary position of the doctrine of the divine origin of the human soul. Catholic theology could never be accused of appealing to the intervention of God without sufficient reason. It was driven to this explanation by the laws of logic. Catholic theology, in this matter of the origin of the human soul, far from ignoring the powers of nature, that begets like from like, clings to those laws longer than does any other philosophy.

This will be seen more clearly if we look for one moment at the argument which forces the theologian to posit a divine origin for the human soul. In a nutshell the argument is as follows. The human soul is an entirely spiritual substance: its activities are far beyond the possibilities of organic matter; organic matter therefore could not be its origin, for an inferior thing cannot be the origin of a vastly superior thing; only a spiritual substance could be the origin of another spiritual substance. As a last resource one might think of the soul of the parent as the origin of the soul of the child; but this could only be conceivable if the parent's soul were divisible into parts, a theory evidently incompatible with the simplicity of a spiritual substance. There being no power either in the body or the soul of the parent to produce a spiritual soul in the offspring, an outside power must be assumed; and this outside power must be one of infinite energy, as it is expected to bring about the existence of a spiritual being from no pre-existing materials.

As I do not profess to write a strictly philosophical treatise, I do not feel bound to reproduce the lengthy and profound reasoning of Saint Thomas Aquinas through which he arrives at the conclusion that God creates every human soul. What I want to impress on the reader is this: if it had been possible to make nature responsible for the existence of every soul, Catholic theologians would have been the last men to doubt her resources. One might almost say that they arrived at their conclusion reluctantly. Nature, in fact, is credited by the Scholastic philosopher with greater powers than by any biologist. His principle is this, that in the production of the human individual nature carries the human organism to such a pitch of perfection as to postulate the active creation of the soul on the part of God, the work of nature being called *passive creation.*

This proposition formulated by Cajetan is worth a moment's meditation. Not only does nature, in the propagation of man, observe all the laws of heredity admitted by biologists, but in man, owing to his superior nature, heredity itself is perfected. Nature produces an organism of such exceeding perfection that it would be a failure unless a spiritual substance were united with it, to which it may minister, so as to have a full scope for its high qualities. The creation of the soul, on the part of God, is not a superseding of nature's activities, it is a completing of her activities. It steps in just where nature falls short, although nature in the production of man, according to our masters, is more marvelous than in the production of any other living being. It shapes an organism which is the appropriate setting for an immortal spirit. Nature fashions the ring of gold, God puts in the brilliant diamond, the soul, in the spot provided by nature.

From this we see how entirely preposterous it would be to consider the creation of the soul as a superfluous hypothesis, heredity being supposed to be resourceful enough to explain everything. Heredity will never explain highest intellectual life and free will.

We take for granted here a clear understanding of creation in the mind of the reader. Creation is not a communication of God's own Personality or Being; creation is the free act of God through which He makes the thing exist without working on pre-existing elements. The human soul is divine in the sense of its being the direct result of God's power. More truly, however, the human soul is divine, because, as spirit, it bears a resemblance to God. Its spirit nature, once more, is to it the source of all greatness.

Before ending, I will deal with a few popular difficulties on the subject.

It would seem as if there were a kind of restriction of God's liberty if He is bound to bring to completion, in the production of man, a work which nature has begun. But all this is strictly in accordance with the universal laws of Providence. God in this case simply carries out His own designs; therefore, His acts, being the sequel of a universal design, are perfectly free acts; God simply does what He willed to do from the very beginning.

This solution is applicable to another difficulty. Would it not seem as if God worked hand in hand with the sinner, when man is conceived through sin? "When nature works at the bidding of sinful instincts, God," says Saint Thomas, "concurs not with sin, but with nature." There is no more reason to be scandalized at this intervention of God's power in man's sin than at His making the sun to rise over the godly and the ungodly. The laws of the universe are of greater importance than man's transitory abuse of free will

Some simple minds might find it difficult to reconcile this constant exercise of God's creative power with their ideas about God's repose. "My Father worketh up to now, and I work," said Incarnate Wisdom. God's repose is His activity, and His activity is His repose. Moreover, the act of God is one unchanging act, without yesterday, or today, or tomorrow; succession is found in the things He creates, not in Himself; for God not only causes things to be, but He causes them to be at such and such a time, to follow upon other events and to prepare the way for things yet to be.

There have been various views among our masters as to the exact moment when the immortal soul is given to the body, through the act of God. The controversy is of little importance; the main point is this: the soul comes only when the organism has reached such a state as to postulate the presence of a higher principle of life.

CHAPTER 12

Creation of the Soul and Heredity

Long before the days of biology, mankind had observed the great phenomenon of natural heredity; the most uneducated will tell you that such and such a quality or defect in your character was your father's or your grandfather's characteristic. Old family friends almost instinctively seek for the explanation of your oddities in your father or grandfather whom they have known. Popular belief in heredity is of a very comprehensive nature; it gives rather more than less. Moral qualities, as well as moral imperfections, are transmitted from parent to child, according to popular opinion.

How then are we to reconcile hereditary acquirements with the advent of the soul from the outside, through creation? Science, as we all know, has followed up the insight of the unsophisticated mind into nature's powers in this matter of heredity. Theology, if anything, would credit nature with more power of transmitting parental qualities than science itself. In fact, theology is ready for any marvel of heredity which scientific observation may bring to light. To quote one instance only: the fallen state of man, if not original sin itself, is entirely an instance of heredity. How then is it that the advent of an immortal soul to the body from the outside does not become to the human individual the beginning of an entirely new state, an entirely new life. Would it not seem that the moment the human embryo is given a spiritual soul it must mean a complete severance from the past, from the exigencies of heredity? Are we not to expect that the immortal soul will be to man not only a principle of higher life, but also a principle of an entirely new life? Are we not to expect that this particular human individual is not what his parents made him, but what the immortal spirit that comes from God makes him?

Our philosophy teaches that there is in man only one soul, the spirit created by God; this one soul is responsible for every kind of activity in man. It is not as if there were a combination of souls, every one of them being the principle of a given form of life, with the spiritual soul at the highest level of them all. The one spiritual soul is the principle and source of every form of life in man.

But this view about the oneness of soul in man seems to create an additional difficulty. For if the one immortal soul in man quickens everything in him, how is there any room left for hereditary qualities, for characteristics which come from the stock from which we spring? Would it not seem that the spiritual soul coming from God should make us all alike through its overwhelming simplicity? Catholic philosophy, as I have already said, is a staunch believer in the powers of heredity. If it had to choose between making the body like unto the soul, or making the soul like unto the body, it would give its preference to the second alternative; that is, it would more readily make the qualities of the body a rule for the soul, than those of the soul a rule for the body. Saint Thomas Aquinas distinctly inclines towards the view that Almighty God fashions the soul He creates according to the body into which He infuses it. As long as the soul's spirituality is safeguarded, there is no reason why the body, with its qualities, should not be to God the occasion for creating a soul with corresponding qualities. This would be merely another application of the principle stated above, that God, in the creation of the soul, follows the predispositions of nature.

However, it is not there that our philosophy looks for the solution of the problem. We do not explain the fact of our being so much the sons of our fathers by saying that God gave us a soul very much in keeping with the qualities and defects left in us by our ancestors, though if we said it, as already remarked, we should not go against the genius of our philosophy. Provided we cling to the spirituality of our soul, we need not fear. There seems to be no contradiction in supposing that spiritual souls may differ widely in qualities, God forming them according to the differences of hereditary dispositions.

Heredity remains entirely unmodified by the quickening action of the immortal soul that comes from God, precisely because it comes to an already constituted organism. The soul does not change that organism, but raises it to a higher life. The soul works on elements already strongly individualized and qualified; in fact, it is against all principles of Scholastic theology to think of an advent of the soul to matter that is crude and lifeless. The immortal soul can be a principle of life only to an organic, living thing; indeed it must find it a living organism when it comes; it makes that living organism do higher things; but the embryonic body cannot be without its initial inherent qualities, as the musician, however perfect in his art, cannot make himself independent of the qualities of his instrument.

It is higher life the soul gives, not new life. This higher life must be carried on with the inherited dispositions, the native qualities. The advent of the immortal soul makes the organism fit for highest love and highest thought; but love and thought in that human individual will be characterized by many predispositions of brain and heart. The soul is indeed the artist; it is even more than the artist: it gives to its instrument the final touch of perfection. However, as the soul is not a creator, but merely a vivifier, it does not make a new instrument, but finishes off a thing half completed by nature.

Nature's work has its qualities and its defects, which the soul cannot change. The soul may add to it a few more strings, but it has still to play on those left by nature. Or better to say, there is not even a new string added to the instrument by the soul; the soul's office is merely to tune all the strings of nature to the highest pitch; but all the tuning in the world will never change the make of the instrument.

Here I must remind the reader of a thing I have said elsewhere, that there are certain intellectual and volitional operations which could never come under the scope of heredity. In those operations all men are equal. Thus all men, whatever their ancestors may have been, see equally clearly the truth of the mathematical statement that two and two are four; all men alike are practically convinced that moral evil is not preferable to moral good. These things come from the spirituality of our soul which is always safeguarded under all possible modifications that come from heredity.

It is there, too, that we shall find an explanation of the problem of which we hear frequently, how man is free in many of his acts, in spite of the predispositions of heredity. Free acts belong to what we call the third region in man, which is quite independent of heredity. It has in fact a certain control over the workings of hereditary dispositions, although the control is far from being complete.

CHAPTER 13

*The Christian Doctrine of the Soul and
Evolutionary Theories of the Descent of Man*

Much has been written about the descent of man. Many a believing Christian has felt keen misgivings when he approached for the first time certain clever books and essays written by the pioneers of evolution, as he felt that they might contain such convincing arguments as to destroy his long-cherished belief in the divine origin of man. Such fears are quite unjustified. For the Christian there cannot be any question about the "Descent of Man," in the sense of the modern controversy. Evolution has no more to do with man's origin, as understood by the Church, than with transubstantiation.

There is only one controversy possible; that which concerns the indwelling of an immortal soul in man. No other question is really of any relevance to the believer. If we are convinced that there is in us an immortal soul, the descent of man becomes essentially an unevolutionist question. If, on the contrary, there be no immortal soul in man, how could we possibly find fault with the evolutionist theory of man's origin? In that case, the evolutionist is the wisest and most spiritual of men.

From the very nature of the subject, evolution can neither prove nor disprove the theory of the indwelling of an immortal soul in man, because the soul begins where evolution ends. Evolution must be, essentially, in the sensitive powers of man, in his organs; the soul is superior to those organs. Evolution cannot be concerned with anything but the organism; a spirit clearly transcends such evolution. Some people seem to think that theories of evolution might demonstrate that there is no immortal soul in man. This no evolution theory is able to do, as evolution is concerned with that part of the history of the human race which is prehistoric, and which therefore does not exhibit traces of any sort of intellectual thought. We can reasonably begin to argue about the existence or nonexistence of the human soul only if we are concerned with a period when thought begins in man. As soon as there is any record of thought, we are in historic times, even if they are called prehistoric by a misuse of language. And by thought I mean here abstract thought, with ratiocination. Such thought, and such thought alone, is an argument in favor of the soul's existence. All controversy, therefore, about the soul's existence must be connected with man's historic life. Whatever went before we may safely leave to the evolutionist; for it is there that he is really at home.

Man has thought through his spiritual soul. He is what he is now, through his immortal soul. This is the Christian position. For the Christian, therefore, the question of man's origin resolves itself into this: how did man become that compound of a spiritual soul with an organic body, which accounts for his life of thought as it is revealed by history? There is no other standpoint for the believer.

To be quite precise, our only enemy is the materialist; the evolutionist, as such, as distinct from the materialist, is the most harmless of men. The evolutionist has not even given new arguments to the materialist, as evolution cannot account for human thought any more than did the materialists in the days before Aristotle.

Where the Christian and the evolutionist might really be on common ground for a controversy is in the interpretation given to the words of Genesis, that God made man, i.e., the body of man, "of the slime of the earth." But evidently, even with that declaration, we know very little as to the way in which the formation of man's body took place, previous to the advent of the immortal soul. That man's body is from the slime of the earth is true in every possible theory.

To sum up. If there is an immortal soul in man, there is no descent of man from imperfect beings, as the immortal soul cannot be evolved. If, on the contrary, there is no immortal soul in man, then, by all means, let us have the Darwinian descent of man. It is quite possible that there may have been beings resembling man much more closely than the modern ape. But without a spiritual soul, they were no more human beings than a frog.

There are people in England who are sincere Christians, or who think themselves to be sincere Christians, without believing in a soul, spiritual and immortal in itself. They are religious oddities; they are the only people who have to dread the modern theories of the descent of Man.

CHAPTER 14

The Mode of Union Between Soul and Body

Our eternal hopes are based on the fact that our soul must have an existence outside the body: when the bodily habitation shall have fallen to pieces the soul goes on living. With this idea of a separate existence for the soul before our eyes, we must now approach the difficult question of the mode of union between soul and body. It is perhaps one of the most subtle concepts in Catholic philosophy, but its subtlety is not such as to prevent the educated lay-mind from arriving at a comparatively clear understanding of it.

I must remark at once that Catholic theology has always steered clear of all theories that make the union between an immortal soul and a bodily organism a kind of penal arrangement, the soul being tied down to a body, for the trespasses of a previous existence. Views of that kind have always possessed a considerable degree of fascination for a certain class of minds. There seems to be something romantic in the idea that the best part of ourselves is a prisoner for deeds done in a higher sphere of the universe. But even discarding all thought of a previous existence, any union between soul and body which would not be a union for the soul's benefit, would be distinctly a most un-Catholic view. Speaking generally, it has simply to be maintained that it is better for the soul to be with the body than to be outside it. We shall try in a subsequent chapter to answer all the objections this assertion might raise.

Granted then the soul's independent existence, and granted the unqualified advantages of the union between soul and body, how are we to conceive that union? Obviously, it must be a union unlike anything else we know from direct observation. For it is not merely a presence of the soul in the body we want, it is a real union between the two. Mere presence, were it ever so beneficial to the body, could never make of soul and body the one being called man. They would always be two distinct beings or personalities; such for instance would be, according to theologians, the presence of an angel, or even an evil spirit, in a bodily being. The two could never make one personality, however long the union might last. We may, of course, as a concession to imaginative thought, consider the soul as having taken up its abode somehow and somewhere inside our bodily frame, and from there ruling and guiding the body; most men will have to be satisfied with that primitive view of the case. It is not a dangerous view so long as it is understood to be merely metaphorical.

Now the philosophical definition of the union between soul and body, which must be called the Catholic definition, as it has become so deeply incorporated into theology, is this: the soul is united with the body, because it is for the human body its Form. No phrase occurs more frequently in the philosophy of past ages; yet if anything ought to surprise us, it is the absence from our modern English usage of this term in its original sense. Everything centers round the significance of the term "form." In the philosophy of past ages Form or *Forma* has inexhaustible metaphysical value. There is no trace of such a great past in the modern "form."

It would be useless for us to proceed, then, unless we succeed in understanding what Form meant to the ancient philosophers and Schoolmen.

These sages started with this principle: in all things created there is composition or duality, the Creator alone being absolutely simple, absolutely one; even the highest spirit is a compound of actuality and potentiality. But confining our attention to the material creation, there we find in every bodily being a duality or composition of Matter and Form. There is in every corporeal being something that is the principle or source of the three dimensions, of inertia, of resistance; and something that is the source or principle of qualities and activities; the first is called Matter; the second is called Form. It will be seen again that Matter, in the philosophical sense, is not quite the same thing as what we should now in everyday language call "matter."

I must be satisfied with this brief sketch of what Matter and Form mean in the old philosophy. For the sake of illustration let me take an example from biology. A plant is built up of elementary substances, easily analyzed by chemistry and expressed in clear formulas. The elements are common elements, found all over nature; they enter into the constitution of many other plants, specifically different from the plant under examination, and even of other beings, as minerals, which are generically different. How is it then that, in this case, those common elements are pressed into service for building up such a being, so different, so individualistic in its nature? There must be at work, in the plant, another principle. Colloquially we should call it the nature of the plant; philosophically we have to call it the Form of the plant. The plant is to be considered as a result, as a product, the product of the special Form, working upon, and utilizing common material elements.

This then is Form; it might also be called soul. There is however this distinction. Even inorganic substances, for instance the chemical elements, are compounds of Matter and Form. Soul is indeed Form, but the Form only of living and sentient beings; in other words, a soul is the same thing as the Form of a living being.

I have not to defend the metaphysical truth of the old Scholastic view of duality in all things created; suffice it to say that it is essentially a point of metaphysics, not a point of experimental science. This duality is not a chemical combination to be verified by a chemical analysis; it is a duality that makes the very existence of a being, and therefore is prior to anything which experimental science could ever submit to its processes.

On the other hand, biology has nothing to fear from the theory of Forms; for with the exception of the human soul all living Forms are said by our masters, and they say it with great emphasis, to be produced by the generative agents from the potentialities of existing Matter. Useless to say that the theory of Matter and Form reaches its noblest applications in the fully developed animal, and the highest among them, man. For no Catholic theologian ever looked askance at the modern phrase that defines man as a highly developed animal. One could fill a book with quotations from Saint Thomas, in which he defines man as a rational animal, *Animal rationale*. This, in fact, is philosophically the only correct definition of man. All other definitions the Scholastic rejects as mere verbiage.

Here, then, the matter under consideration is brought to a clear issue: the thing that is Form to the human organism and makes the human animal the perfect sentient being it is, such as we know it, is the immortal soul created by God, a spirit, as we have said, that is at the same time soul. In other words, the spirit of man is able to fulfill the functions of Form, though it has also higher functions than mere Form-functions, to which it is by no means confined. The soul, then, is united with the body as Form is united with Matter, and in this, and in this alone, consists the wonderful union. The human soul is Form, but it is a Form that rises above Matter, and in this superiority to Matter it differs from all other Forms.

No doubt endless questions could be asked here; how, for instance, it all coincides with heredity on the one hand, and the advent of the soul from the outside on the other, for the human soul comes from God, not from the parents. But this is not the chapter for such questions. What I undertook to explain here, I think I have shown satisfactorily, namely, the mode of union between body and soul.

CHAPTER 15

The Soul's Existence

It may surprise the reader to find that I have kept until now the answer to the most crucial of all questions, whether there is such a thing as a soul in man. But there is something to be said in favor of my arrangement. Most of the arguments against the existence of the soul come from ignorance of the soul's nature. The chapters that precede have given to the reader such views of the soul that I may confidently hope his mind is now prepared for the positive proofs of the soul's existence.

What is called science cannot in any way formulate a reasonable objection against the possibility of there being spirits, or more particularly, of there being such a spirit as the human soul. The existence, or nonexistence, of entirely spiritual beings cannot in any way belong to science, as science is based entirely on observable data, and spirits, from the very fact of their being spirits, cannot come under man's observation. The existence of spirits must belong therefore entirely to Faith; and nothing could be more idle than to invoke the pronouncements of science either for or against the existence, or even the possibility, of spirits.

But the question assumes quite a different aspect if we put it like this: Is there such a spirit present in, and united with, the human body? This has nothing in common with the other question, whether there are spirits. There may be, or may not be, such things as birds with feathers of celestial blue; I cannot pronounce against the possibility of there being somewhere such specimens of the feathered world. But of this I can judge with certainty; whether a bird of that kind is actually in my garden. Is there, then, actually at this moment, an immaterial spirit residing in my body? Put in that way, the question is well-expressed, and deserves a reasonable answer. All controversies, therefore, between materialists and believers must be brought back to this point: are there evidences of the presence of an immaterial spirit in man's body? Or are there, on the contrary, clear proofs that there is no such spirit in man?

Our masters in sacred theology have a twofold basis on which to establish an argument that leads up to the admission of an entirely spiritual principle in man: a soul. Their first basis is the wonderfully high sensitive life in man. Their second basis is the existence in our minds of Universals, a term soon to be explained.

Sensitive life in man has an incomparably wide range and rises to an extraordinary level. Think of aesthetic pleasures, and the higher manifestations of sexual and maternal instincts, which yet do not go beyond sensitive life. They are the things of the body. Now, what our masters say is this: between man and the higher animals, the organic differences are not such as to account for those enormous differences in feeling and loving. The organisms may be nearly the same; but in the end-results of their functions the superiority on the side of man is so great that one has to look for something that is not mere organism. And that something is the spiritual soul "raising up" the common organism to higher activities. It is, in fact, the "elevation" of the organism by the soul, of which Saint Thomas speaks so often. Man's organs not being such as to explain the enormous advances in feeling and love which he enjoys, modern materialists, unwilling to admit the spiritual soul, have invented fantastic theories to account for this high level of sensitive life in man. But human organs act so perfectly, because they are "leavened" by a spiritual soul.

The second basis for establishing the presence of the spiritual soul within us is constituted by the Universals. I say, for instance, "Where is gratitude?" This term, "gratitude," is a Universal, because it represents a notion that is applicable universally, without limits. Gratitude is an idea which is representative of a thing that is not confined to any time, to any place. Now, say our masters, a conscious being that can think in Universals must be a spiritual, a non-material being. It must be above the limitations of matter, otherwise it could not conceive ideas that are applicable in every possible sphere. On Universals is based the power of abstract reasoning. Just think of the endless applicability of this idea of gratitude! Think of its possibilities for ratiocination!

If we turn now to the objections that are brought forward against the existence of a spiritual soul in man, we find that they all center round the dependence of the supposed spirit-life on bodily organs and conditions. The materialist argues thus: Man's intellectual life entirely depends on the state of the brain. An immature, or defective, or infirm brain is an immature, defective, or infirm intellectual life. Is it not tantamount to blasphemy to suppose a mighty being, such as an immaterial spirit must be, present in a child, in an old man struck with senile decay, in the mentally deranged, and condemned to be a silent, idle spectator of his sad failure or suffering? A small dose of anaesthetic may bring a total suspension of all that wonderful mental life. Science can easily explain how the beneficent gas interrupts thought and will-functions. How is it possible then to maintain the existence of a totally spiritual principle? Surely gas has no hold on a spirit! Therefore, though we cannot explain the higher feeling and higher thought in man, we can at least show evidence that this thought and love are the captives of merely chemical activities, which surely proves that they cannot be spirit-manifestations!

Our answer is easy from all that precedes. We say that we supposed all along precisely those things that are a stumbling block to the materialist. Those very considerations are part and parcel of our theory of man's spiritual soul. The delays, and cessations, and modifications in the intellectual life, in many cases traceable so directly to mere organic causes, far from telling against the presence of a spiritual substance in man, are, on the contrary, inevitable corollaries of such a presence. I would not go so far as to say that they are a clear evidence of that presence; this they are not, and cannot be; but what I say is this, that these phenomena are not only no proof against the soul's presence, but are just what we would expect to happen if there be a spiritual soul in man.

The principal mission of the soul, its raising up of the senses, supposes senses in a normal state. It is the very opposite of the condition of itself being able to be raised. A brain in an abnormal state is no more fit to be raised by the soul to higher life than is a broken instrument fit to be made to sound harmoniously, even by the perfect musician. If there be present in man an entirely spiritual substance, separable from the body, then it becomes absolutely necessary that things should be with regard to our brain functions just as experience shows.

Most men look exclusively at the fact of spirituality; it is the one thing that fascinates them, while it repels them by its apparent impossibility. Now this is to look in the wrong direction; this is to shy at the wrong object. There is no difficulty here, nothing we could reasonably take exception to, as just said. Why should there be no such thing as spiritual substances? Or, anyhow, why not leave their existence peacefully to the region of possibilities?

The paramount question is not about the fact of a spiritual substance, but about the *presence* of such a substance in my body. How is it possible that such a substance should be present in my body, should be united with it? The whole controversy must be about the *presence*, not the spirituality as such. "I cannot reconcile such a presence with those well-known suspensions of intellectual life in man," you may say. My answer is this: such a presence not only may be reconciled with these interruptions of intellectual life, but it actually supposes them; it is entirely compatible with them.

What does it mean when we say that a spiritual soul is present in the body? Being a spirit, it is not inside the body as a chair is in a room. Its presence necessarily connotes action of some kind; on the part of the soul upon the body, and on the part of the body upon the soul. This interaction and mutual influence form the bond of union, and are the only possible connection to be thought of when we speak of the soul's presence in the body.

By every law, if the soul had one single action absolutely independent of the body, it would no longer be in the body. We may speak of the soul as rising above bodily action, we never speak of the soul's independence of bodily influence.

There is a great difference between the presence of an angel and the presence of a human soul. The angel may work upon an object, say the iron door of Saint Peter's prison; he is really there, precisely because he is working there, is exerting his power there; but he could never be said to be one person with this material object.

But the action of the soul is so intimate, so wedded with the bodily organs on which it is exercised, as to involve vital reaction on the part of the body, and to knit soul and body into one person. Should, therefore, the human body elicit even one of its human acts without the cooperation of the soul, soul and body would no longer be mated so as to form one person; and should the soul perform one single act without the cooperation of the body, the union would have been severed.

Without in the least doubting the immaterial character of our higher or universal thoughts, our masters insist on our seeing how these very thoughts, the moment they exist, are conditioned primarily by sense-operations. Intellectual work, even of the highest kind, is invariably brain-work, with all its fatigues and eclipses; not, indeed, in the sense that everything ends in brain-activity, but in the sense that the brain is busily engaged in supplying the non-organic, non-brain-bound intellect with the elements for Universals, for its unlimited, immaterial notions. For we must remember that the presentment of material objects to the immaterial mind is necessary at every stage of the mental work. The intellect never retains notions once received, but always gets them directly from the senses whenever it works, though it may work in a way so marvelous that the senses cannot approach it in point of perfection. The mind, therefore, is a blank at every period of its existence, unless it be stimulated, and fed by the senses.

This is the Scholastic view of the intellectual function, and it shows well how the immaterial mind is subject to organic conditions, being indebted to them for the elements of its knowledge. If soul and body are supposed to make one person, their union can only last so long as they work with each other in every act;

and the more there is of mutual work, the more intimate is that union. The superior part of man, the soul, is kept united to the inferior part, the body, only through that interdependence of activities.

The Catholic standpoint, therefore, is that man cannot be explained without the hypothesis of an entirely spiritual principle, united, in some very intimate way with the bodily organism. It is a theological proposition which cannot be controverted by a Catholic, that man, through his intellectual and volitional life, gives evidences of there being in him a principle of activities superior to the possibilities of organic matter.

It is not maintained, however, that every human individual manifests such evidences of a higher principle as to enable a philosopher to conclude that in this particular individual there is an immortal soul. Saint Thomas admits the difficulty of that mental analysis by which the philosopher ultimately distinguishes spiritual operations from organic operations; the difficulty is owing to the wonderful and almost inexhaustible resourcefulness of organic life. If this is the case with the normally constituted human organism, how much more difficult will it be to find in the organically debased, or the organically imperfect, evidences of a spiritual soul.

But in order to give a true definition of man one need not stop short at the imperfect specimens of the race. One ought to take the perfect specimens as the normal representatives of the type; and if those perfect specimens have such activities as to exact the hypothesis of a spiritual soul, we must admit the soul for the whole species, as a spiritual soul is quite compatible with a low state of individual development (as discussed in Chapter 7).

My contention here is simply this, that there may be human beings in whom, owing to abnormal conditions, there are no clear signs of activities of either of the two orders set forth in this chapter, I mean the higher sensitive life and the purely intellectual life. I maintain, besides, that with some people, in whom there is a higher sensitive life, the purely intellectual life may not be very evident. But this does not weaken the standpoint of Catholic theology. All we need to hold, in order to be in conformity with theology, is the fact that mankind, as a whole, gives evidences of such activities as to postulate the hypothesis of a spiritual soul united to the human organism.

I have not treated of the moral proofs in favor of the existence of the human soul. The tradition of mankind, revealed faith, man's higher aspirations, I call the moral proofs. They are, in reality, the most weighty arguments with most men. These proofs stand on their own merits, and do not come within our present scope; all we need do here is to show how man's observable psychology does not reveal anything irreconcilable with the conclusions arrived at through those moral proofs. If my reasonings show anything, they should show clearly how much more difficult it is to explain man without the hypothesis of a spiritual principle, than to admit the presence of such a principle.

CHAPTER 16

The Human Soul at its Separation from the Body

There are few things in theology that are of greater personal interest to each of one us than the conditions of existence for the human soul the moment it departs from the body. It is of course a hard task for our imagination to picture to itself the great tragedy of that parting between soul and body; it is only theological considerations that can give rest and satisfaction to the mind in this matter.

Death would be badly defined if we defined it as a separation of soul and body. The soul need not be considered at all in the study of the phenomenon of death. What we have to consider are the causes, physical and otherwise, that bring about the breaking up of the human organism. The materialist makes himself ridiculous when he pretends to do away with the soul because he is able to explain death without being obliged to have recourse to the departure of the soul. There might be a thousand souls in a human body and death would still occur, as it occurs now, through laws that physical observation may follow almost to their source. The office of the soul has never been understood by our masters otherwise than as a power of elevation, making our organism do what it could not do if it were left to mere animal vitality.

The destruction therefore of the organism, which it is as easy to explain as it is to effect, makes the soul lose its hold on the body. Being a spirit, its only tie to the body is its activity in the body, or at least its influence on the body. By influence I mean those results in the bodily organism which I have described in the chapters on Elevation, and on the Mode of Union between Soul and Body. This activity having been rendered impossible through the failing of the organism, the soul's presence in the body is at an end. Spirit-like, it passes into an entirely new state. We need not think of it as being carried away by an angel, or a demon, into a distant world of spirits; we need not think of it as flying there through its own activity, or even as being placed there by the hand of God. All these expressions are useful metaphors, of course, but only metaphors. It simply passes from activity in the body into the spirit-state, good or evil, happy or unhappy, according to its will-dispositions. It is in Heaven, or it is in Hell, or in some other state proper to a spirit, through no longer being an active power in the human organism.

We say of an angel that for him to be on earth is to have a beneficent influence on a person or a place on this earth. When the influence ceases he is no longer on earth through the very fact of that cessation of influence. If it were necessary for the human soul, once separated, to have active influence on a given part of the material universe, or to be influenced by it passively, it would find itself there, through a kind of spirit-mobility which is given to it as a congenial attribute of its new state. But its transference into the spirit-world is effected, as I have said, through the cessation of its activity on the body.

One consideration that finds its place here is this: whatever knowledge the disembodied spirit may possess of the affairs of this world, there is one impediment that does not exist for it—distance in space. Geographical remoteness or proximity has absolutely nothing to do with the matter of spirit-knowledge; and if spirits ignore what happens on earth, they do not do so because they are far from it, but for other reasons.

Catholic theology has assimilated what was best in all human philosophies, and has fought its battles side by side with the keenest minds not enlightened by Faith. The Arabs of the thirteenth century, on the Spanish peninsula, had built up on the old Greek philosophies a magnificent system, partly intellectual, partly religious, which comes next in dignity to Scholastic theology. They discussed all the questions which our own masters studied and solved. In this matter of the soul, in a state of separation from the body, they had a very plausible and a very alluring theory. They considered that the soul, by passing into the spirit-state, had reached its final state, its ultimate perfection; that its union with the body was rather an impediment to its perfection, and therefore separation was the thing to be desired. Saint Thomas always fought shy of this facile explanation of the condition of the separated soul. For him the state of separation is never an absolute perfection, is never the final repose of the soul. He always considers that the union between soul and body is for the benefit of the soul, and that separation means loss to the soul as well as to the body.

This, of course, is to be understood apart from any supernatural privileges.

On the other hand, Saint Thomas is not less emphatic and insistent in teaching that, at death, the soul enters into a spirit-state which it did not possess before. There seems, therefore, to be an apparent contradiction in his teaching, a contradiction that is not found in the theories of the Arab philosophers. This difficulty is still more emphasized by our Doctor's own teaching about the knowledge communicated to the separated soul, which according to him is mediated through the instrumentality of higher spirits. A vision of the whole material universe; a clear perception of its own self as a spirit, which it did not possess in life; and finally, an at least approximate knowledge of the angelic nature in general: such is the intellectual equipment of the separated soul, good or bad. In a word, Saint Thomas constantly teaches that separation means the turning of the human intellect towards higher things, while in a state of union with the body it is turned towards lower things. Nor does he consider the state of the separated soul as being an anti-natural state, a violent, contradictory state. He only calls it a preternatural state, that is to say, a state which is not contemplated originally by Nature, but which, when it comes, is not one of suffering or privation, unless there be moral guilt in the soul. With all this, I say, it seems difficult to understand his doctrine that the union between soul and body is for the good of the soul, and that the separation is after all a loss.

There would be one answer, to begin with, which might be at least a partial solution of the apparent contradiction. The knowledge poured into the separated soul, by the higher spirits, is a universal, vague knowledge, containing no particular, definite facts; it would require supernatural privileges to enter into the facts of the spirit-world; and happiness of thought does not come through a vague, abstract knowledge, but through the knowledge of the living fact.

This the soul receives through bodily senses here in life. In the state of separation, the soul has higher knowledge, but no explicit knowledge of individual facts, except of a limited number. In the state of union we only know lower things, but we know them explicitly in their own particular mode; and this is the kind of knowledge that makes us happy, while the other knowledge seems only to create a great desire and craving for the explicit, individual fact. Yet, to my mind, this would not fully establish the superiority of the state of union over that of separation. I offer therefore the following solution. It is better for the soul to be separated from the body, as the body is now, after the Fall; a body entirely left to its organic resources, without any higher gifts from God. But it is a great loss to the soul to be separated from the body, as God made it first, in the state of innocence; as God will make it in the final resurrection, or anyhow, as God might make it, even now, if there were not the curse of original sin. United with bodies of that kind, the soul would have perceived the facts and events that occur in the material world and at the same time would have contemplated the higher, the spiritual things.

But with our present supernatural privileges of soul it is a decided gain for the soul to be separated from the body. "For to me, to live is Christ, and to die is gain. And if to live in the flesh, this is to me the fruit of labor, and what I shall choose I know not. But I am straitened between two, having a desire to be dissolved and to be with Christ, a thing by far the better" (Philippians 1:21–23). "For we know, if our earthly house of this habitation be dissolved, that we have a building of God, a house not made with hands, eternal in heaven. For in this also we groan, desiring to be clothed upon with our habitation that is from heaven. ... For we also, who are in this tabernacle, do groan, being burdened, because we would not be unclothed, but clothed upon, that that which is mortal may be swallowed up by life" (2 Corinthians 5:1, 2, 4). Under the present dispensation the body has no supernatural privileges while the soul is full of them. When therefore the soul will be alone, in the state of separation, her life will be a higher and happier life than it is now, being united with a body destitute of supernatural qualities. The happiest state, of course, will be the union of the glorified soul with a glorified body.

The one principle which Saint Thomas wanted to save is this: that man is completely and perfectly man, and therefore fully capable of human happiness, only when he is composed of soul and body; a principle which the Arabian philosophers denied. But he does not maintain that this is the case under every possible condition; there is at least one possibility for the human soul to be happier outside the body than in it. It is, as I have said, the condition of those in whom the soul is highly privileged, while the body remains a body of sin.

CHAPTER 17

The Knowledge of the Disembodied Soul

At death the wall of flesh that has hidden the spirit crumbles away; the soul finds itself forever in the spirit-world, where all is will and intellect, where sunrise is intellectual illumination and sunset the withholding of further knowledge; where cold and heat are fixities of purpose and will-activities. And here we must remember that this new condition of things is practically independent of the intellectual development of the soul's existence in the body; I mean precisely intellectual as distinct from moral development. The souls of children who left this life before they could distinguish their right hand from their left form a vast company. They enjoyed no intellectual development in their mortal days. Yet those souls are not more tenuous or smaller than the soul of the man who found out the laws of universal gravitation. In the state of separation, both "big and small" are equally exposed to the penetrating rays of the spirit-world.

How are souls raised to spirit-life? How do they get spirit-knowledge? The theory of Saint Thomas about the way a disembodied human soul acquires spirit-knowledge is wonderfully bold; at the same time it is exceedingly simple.

The whole spirit-world constantly radiates knowledge, as the material world sends forth the stimuli of our senses. Spirits are incessantly at work, they never rest; and their activity is to impart knowledge.

Every spirit receives those communications in a measure dependent on his own capacity, his own power of grasping the thought. Nor is it in the power of a spirit to screen himself from the influence of those communications.

The disembodied soul is thus filled with wide and sublime knowledge, as the bodily eye, when open, is filled with the vision of all that lies within its horizon.

There is no distinction in this matter between holy and reprobate souls, for those spirit-communications are a law of their nature; they become the happiness of the upright, and the despair of the perverted will.

The elect soul, of course, will be the object of further illumination of a higher order. But we are speaking in this chapter of the merely natural conditions, not of the privileged condition of the soul.

As a corollary of this doctrine of the knowledge-giving activities of the spirit-world, the Angelic Doctor says that every human soul, the moment it is separated from the body, has a full and complete knowledge of the material universe and its laws, besides a general knowledge of the spirit-universe. This second kind of knowledge, however, is less distinct and explicit than the first. The material world and its laws are something lower than the human soul; the soul, therefore, is equal to the task of comprehending them. Spirits properly so called are above the soul, and the soul is unequal to the task of comprehending them.

It may be difficult for us to realize that in the degraded, besotted tramp we see lying on the roadside there is a soul of such vast capacity that it would only take a small dose of poison administered to the body to make the soul live a colossal spirit-life. Yet nothing short of this view, so constantly inculcated by our masters in theology, will give us the reason why the Son of God died on the Cross. God could not die for anything small.

The question will be asked, no doubt: Why does this illumination of the human soul take place only after its separation from the body? Why should the body cover the soul "as with a sack of hair-cloth" to intercept spirit-illumination? Why should it be impossible for the activities of the spirit-world to penetrate through our bodily tissues, to reach the soul while it is in the body?

The answer of Saint Thomas is simple in the extreme, so simple indeed that some might feel tempted to ask for deeper doctrine. While in the body, he says, the soul is *effusa*, spread throughout the body; it exhausts itself in being the leavening, the elevating principle of our bodily frame. In this activity, if activity it may be called, it has no perception for higher spirit-influence. In other words (and this may have the appearance of being more learned than the simple words of Aquinas) there is a certain readiness of perception required in order that the soul may be benefited by the spirit-world activities; this perceptiveness the human soul does not possess here on earth, through the very fact of its being so preoccupied with the task of giving higher life to the body. In order that a brain should be able to function as our brain does, a spirit must spend itself in being its "psychic leaven."

Our philosophy is far from being niggardly in this matter of spirit-knowledge for the disembodied human soul. But we shall discuss presently the question of how it is that, after all, separation from the body is not an unmixed happiness for the soul, in spite of this flood of new knowledge.

Happiness comes from the rectitude of the spirit-will; knowledge alone, unless it be of the secrets of God, is indifferent material for spirit-happiness.

CHAPTER 18

The State of the Soul

There is one conclusion, the practical importance of which is enormous, that follows from the absolute immateriality of the disembodied human soul. Having realized the utter detachment of the disembodied human soul from matter, time and space, we ask ourselves this question, with a kind of awe: how then do souls differ among themselves? What makes them of high or low degree?

For the soul we have not got the specific differentiation that makes of every angel another star in the spirit-world. All human souls are fundamentally equal in spirit-rank.

The answer is this: It is the moral state of the soul that matters: the soul is differentiated through its moral state; it is high or low through that state, when all differentiations of matter, time and space are gone. The moral state of the soul will be its wings or its burden.

As our masters say so shrewdly, the disembodied soul passes without any local movement from the state of soul into the state of pure spirit, and the distance traveled in that simple change of state is almost infinite. But the spirit-state itself is conditioned by the moral state, and so the change is a passing without local displacement, into eternal sanctity or eternal sin.

We have to consider here the state of the soul as it is at the very last instant of its union with the body; it is called a state because it is a real, permanent, deeply engraved molding of the soul, not merely transitory acts and emotions. The human soul makes for itself, acquires for itself, a permanent moral attitude or character, which, united with sanctifying grace, establishes it in its spiritual stature. Now this state is not given; it is acquired through a succession of personal acts. The reason is obvious. Every being has proper activity; the higher the being, the higher the activity. Among terrestrial beings the human soul is the highest; therefore it must have highest activity, and its perfection or state will be the result of its own activities cooperating with God's grace.

And here I should like to speak of a subject that lies near to my heart. Our lot is cast with a generation which idolizes action and activity. But through an inexplicable contradiction, though perhaps a searcher of the heart would not think it a contradiction, spiritual activity and enterprise are not popular. We live with men who are tossed about by every wind of doctrine in the things of the spirit; and yet their minds and hearts do not suffer from the uncertainty; they consider that God, who has made them what they are, will make it all right in the end. Why should they strive after spiritual truth and perfection? They have lost the old Christian conviction of the importance of the moral state of the soul; for their naive expectation of a gratuitous action of God, that would come in and mend matters when needed, is no moral perfection. It is no step towards acquiring a moral state; it is repose and stagnation in spiritual things. Such an attitude, though it be that of many an honest Englishman, is quite indefensible. It has no parallel in all we know of the laws of God and the world. In nature all is activity; and what is more, a specific result is always the fruit of some specific activity. There are normally no substitutes for the activities of natural powers. In the lives of human beings, disadvantages of birth, of mind, or of body, are not made good by an extraordinary providence; they, may be corrected to a great extent by greater personal effort, they are seldom corrected by extraordinary providence.

As a matter of fact, in their practical lives, both social and economic, men do not consider that a disadvantage in which they are placed, and which is not of their own doing, is a sufficient reason for settling down to its inconveniences. If they do so resign themselves, it will be said by all thoughtful men that they have only themselves to blame for being hindmost in the race. It is only when they come to what vitally concerns the soul, the highest part of man, that men appear to reason differently, and bring themselves to believe that spiritual or religious disadvantages need not make them enterprising, need not send them off to search for what is good and true. There is surely no justification for this comfortable acquiescence in what, after all, is spiritual poverty.

If we turn to the Bible, England's greatest heritage, is not its genius essentially one of spiritual enterprise, proclaiming the search for truth and sanctity man's first duty? There is no one more lenient with regard to the eternal fate of the non-Catholic than the Catholic theologian. He knows how to draw the distinction between culpable and unavoidable error. One of the first distinctions with which the young student in theology is made acquainted is the distinction between *ignorantia vincibilis* and *ignorantia invincibilis*, ignorance that may be overcome, and ignorance that cannot be overcome.

"To err is human"; But lack of solicitude for his eternal welfare, and for the means of bringing it about, is moral deformity. The very effort to strive after truth is a high moral act; it shapes the soul, even if the truth cannot be found; and great will be the mercies meted out to the humble inquirer.

CHAPTER 19

Virtue, the Soul's Greatness

It is a principle of Catholic theology, the importance of which cannot be exaggerated, that a spirit's status with God depends entirely on the psychological properties it possesses.

We are in the eyes of God what we are in ourselves; if we are great before God, we are great through qualities which are an inherent property of our own personality. There is no such thing as mere external imputation of any dignity or state or sanctity on the part of God. "Imputation" is a term fabricated by the Reformers of the sixteenth century. According to them, man can have no inherent quality that makes him into a saint; he is radically unfit for it; but God looks upon him as a holy being out of consideration for Christ's sanctity. This is called justification or sanctity by imputation. I quote this tenet of reforming theology as a principle referring not only to sanctification, but to every possible branch of moral elevation. Such imputation on the part of God is repulsive to Catholic theology; it is an unreality, a sham unworthy of eternal Truth.

Whatever dignity we have in the spirit-world is always and everywhere a greatness of mind and of will. It might truly be said that the Catholic theology of justification and sanctification is all psychological. The wonderful work of Redemption results in ever so many psychological effects for the human individual. Redemption is not just a great spiritual drama to be looked at and admired; it is a great spiritual power that is to transform individual souls, to make them live a higher life. Catholic theology is not surprised at any height of supernatural psychological perfection to which a human soul may be raised through the active operation of Redemption.

The soul of the redeemed is a holy thing, a thing full of spiritual excellences, a marvel to God's angels, a terror to the spirits of darkness, a living temple of the Holy Spirit, a vessel of election full of the sweetness of the Spirit of God. This is a view of which the orthodox Protestant is entirely destitute. For him Redemption is the gratuitous saving of the unworthy, remaining in his state of unworthiness. He knows nothing of the exhilarating beauties of the sanctified soul, that make it a thing full of grace and loveliness to God Himself. The Protestant makes of salvation a transaction entirely external to man, while, in the eyes of the Catholic, man is saved only when his soul is beautiful and strong.

I said that all our worth in the eyes of God is greatness either of mind or of will. Greatness of mind is the reward, greatness of will is the merit.

This is why Catholic theology attaches so much importance, both in theory and in practice, to virtue; for virtue is the greatness of the will both in time and in eternity. Virtues are the ornament of the soul, its greatness, its royal priesthood, its nobility; virtues, from the very fact of being virtues, are what we might call the most subjective portion of the spirit; they become part and parcel of the spirit itself.

It is true that some virtues are given to the soul by God; but that endowment does not make them less the soul's property residing in the innermost sources of its being; for it is in the power of God, who created the spirit, and gave it its individuality, to bestow on it new and higher qualities that make it greater and stronger. God is able, and He alone is able, to give new qualities to a spirit, which yet are part of what is most vital to it. God alone can enter into the depths of our being, and there deposit new seeds that spring up into the soul's own eternal life.

A great man once said that, to him, the *Summa* of Saint Thomas was a greater epic than Homer's *Odyssey*; so likewise the vicissitudes of virtue in a soul are the only dramas and tragedies worthy of our interest. It is there where the spirit stands and falls, and where the world is eternally divided.

CHAPTER 20

The Body's Share in Spiritual Life

Spiritual life is not the same thing as spirit-life. Spirit-life is in the activities of a pure spirit; spiritual life may be found in activities that are bodily activities.

Spiritual life as distinguished from spirit-life is found in man only; there is no such distinction possible with the pure disembodied spirit. A spirit's life may be a holy or an unholy life; it may be a happy or an unhappy life, but it could not be called a spiritual or unspiritual life.

Spiritual life is primarily bodily life, but bodily life that is for the benefit of the spirit, the human soul. Nothing would be more dangerous than to make spiritual life consist exclusively in the spirit-acts of the soul, if there be any such acts in mortal life. Such a definition would exclude from spiritual life that part of man which is most obvious and most directly present to him, his bodily senses. Spiritual life is the life of the body, the life of the senses shaped in such a fashion as to be both worthy of, and beneficial to, the soul. If spiritual life were to consist exclusively of the spirit-acts of the soul, the greatest portion of our activities in this mortal existence would at once be outside the pale of spirituality.

Catholicism is the most spiritual religion in the world, yet Catholicism has never found it necessary to condemn the body as an obstacle to spiritual life. Catholic philosophy, on the contrary, has made the soul's progress depend on the soul's union with the body.

There is no spiritual life after the separation of soul and body; it will then be spirit-life, happy or unhappy, holy or unholy. The old Christian doctrine that all growth in sanctity ceases with death ought at once to make us realize what share the body must have in spiritual life.

Now it is against the very genius of Catholic spirituality to consider that the cessation in the power of meriting, or rather of growing in virtue, is an arbitrary disposition of Providence. God deals with His creatures according to their nature, and He never takes away from them any powers or potentialities of which they may be possessed. Whatever happens to the soul happens as a result of its own inherent laws. Therefore the cessation for the soul of growth in spiritual perfection, which, as we have said, is the result of the separation of the soul from the body, must come exclusively from the death of the body; in other words, the body is the intrinsic, necessary, and indispensable condition of growth in spiritual perfection.

All this points to a profound truth: spiritual life is the highest moral life of the body.

Such a view of spiritual life ought to be welcome to man, as his soul is something far too hidden, far too difficult to seize upon. Its very existence is brought home to him only through elaborate reasonings. If spiritual life were defined as the life of the spirit, it ought at once to be classed among the unfeasible, the impracticable things; far from its being man's daily and hourly aim, it could not be anything but an exceptional state.

Every act of spiritual life requires the activity of our senses, or anyhow the concurrence of our senses. First there is a vast amount of spiritual activity which is done directly by the senses. Secondly, even those acts that approach most nearly to pure spirit-life are not possible without the concurrence of the senses, for the same reasons that make thought and will in us universally dependent on the cooperation of the senses. Thirdly, all the external results of our internal sanctity are dependent on our sense-activities, and those sense-activities are practically the only reliable tokens of the sincerity of the more hidden dispositions of our will, or of our soul.

To give instances; all those attractive and ennobling virtues that may be classed under the heading of purity, and which contribute so much towards our spirituality, are the work of our senses. It is the body that is chaste; it is the body that is temperate. The soul alone could not be said to have habits of that kind, except metaphorically, from the very fact of its being a spirit.

Strength and courage are another class of virtue with many subdivisions. Now strength and courage are again bodily dispositions; only metaphorically could the soul alone be said to possess such virtues.

On the other hand, prayer, the intimate conversation of the soul with God, is an activity that is more spirit-like. Yet even prayer is not possible without the constant concurrence of our higher senses, our imaginative and affective powers.

Religion of the heart would be a most uncertain virtue if it did not express itself in external worship, in the praise of the lips, in the reverence of the body.

Nothing would be easier than to survey all the virtuous acts and dispositions of man; and it would be found invariably that they are either virtuous dispositions of the senses themselves, or acts of the soul which are impossible without the concurrence of the senses, or acts whose very sincerity requires external bodily manifestation.

We are right therefore in saying that for all practical purposes spiritual life is not so much spirit-life, as the higher life of the body. Spiritual life is the highest and noblest way the body has of asserting itself. To speak of spiritual life as the life that does not take count of the body, if anything be meant by such a phrase, is the direct contradiction of traditional Catholic spirituality.

Asceticism has held, and still holds, too important a place in the Christian, or at least in the Catholic, view of life to be omitted in a treatise on the human soul. The subject follows naturally the considerations we have just made, on the body's share in spiritual life. We said that spiritual life gives to the body its best opportunity of asserting itself. Would it not appear as if the importance attached in Catholicism to asceticism hardly bears out this assertion? I willingly confess that nothing would be easier than to fill a volume with quotations from orthodox writers preaching, in every kind of language, the destruction of the body of sin. A Buddhist who seeks after spiritual life through the extinction of bodily activity might easily quote Christian writers with a view to justifying his conduct. The saints have done and said hard things against the body; they have called the body their greatest enemy, to which there ought to be no quarter given. How are we to reconcile that incessant wailing over the body's iniquities, that desperate persecution of the body, with the view that the body finds in spiritual life its best chance for asserting itself?

Now I make so bold as to say that a certain amount of Christian language in this matter of mortification is both metaphorical and hyperbolic. I will go further and say that, besides exaggerated language, there has been occasionally, or even frequently, exaggerated practice in individual cases. The Church is not responsible for the over-fervid behavior of some of her best children.

Mortification is the outcome of courage, and, like courage, it has a tendency to strike too hard, to degenerate into foolhardiness. Owing to the limitations of our nature even our virtues cast shadows. We suffer from our own perfections, and the brave man may easily become an intolerant man. It will be useful, in daily life, to remember that the possession of one virtue does not mean all-round perfection. We need not hesitate to make these concessions to truth, as there has always been in the Church of God a clear body of teaching concerning the role of asceticism. We might call it the Church's official doctrine on mortification. The Church has never erred through excess in that matter; if anything, the Church has curbed the ardor of the saint and the ascetic.

There is perhaps hardly a subject, in the practical order of things, in which heresy would be easier, than in this subject of mortification. And heresies there have been, because nothing looks so much like virtue as man's hardness with his own body, since most men sin, and are known by all men to be sinners, through their indulgence of the body.

Asceticism, in the Catholic sense, is essentially the assertion of the body, not its negation. The aim of asceticism is to strengthen virtue. The Church never took any other view of it. Now virtue is in the senses; it is the highest perfection of the senses; it is purity and strength of character. Mortification is to deaden, or to curb, not the senses, but those unruly appetites that weaken the sense of purity, that weaken the moral fiber of man. To make a man pure and to make a man strong, such is the aim of mortification. To repress anything, to abstain from anything, without that end in view is not a virtuous act, but an unwise act, an imprudent act, an act that is against reason.

But there is a difficulty here.

It is comparatively easy to know what kind of abnegations foster purity and modesty, foster the dignity of the human body; but it would appear that there is no limit to the exercise of fortitude, which is another word for strength of character. In order to become strong, shall we not afflict our body without interruption and without mercy? For would it not seem that he is strongest who can hold out longest? On these grounds it would appear that there is no limit to mortification.

Our masters have provided us with the answer to this dangerous sophistry.

Man is not made perfect directly through bearing hard things. Sin and its consequences, sooner or later, are the hardest things to bear, and yet they leave man in his state of depravity. To bear a hard thing does not make man strong; but to bear a hard thing, which is at the same time a wise thing, makes him strong. Only such hardships create moral strength as are necessary in order to do what wisdom and prudence command. As Saint Augustine says, it is not death, but it is the cause for which he dies, that makes the martyr.

There is, however, in Catholic sanctity a sacrifice of the body which could not be called mortification, though it resembles mortification. It is not intended as a safeguard of purity, as an exercise of courage, but as a holocaust to God, as a sacrifice, as an atonement for personal sin, or for the sins of mankind. Such are the most adorable of all sufferings, the sufferings of Christ on the Cross.

Sufferings of that kind do not come under the heading of mortification, because their explanation is more theological than psychological. There have been sufferings of that kind in the lives of the saints, whose desire it was to resemble Christ crucified, to renew in their bodies the Passion of Christ.

Such sufferings need not alarm us; it is part of their purpose to be according to the dictates of wisdom. Christ suffered as much as the Father in His wisdom had exacted; and when He had fulfilled the measure, He pronounced His *Consummatum est*. So likewise the saint, in imitation of his crucified Savior, will keep the measure of wisdom, even in the eager generosity of his love.

CHAPTER 21

Mortal Sin, the Evil of the Soul

A Catholic instinctively thinks of sin as the evil of the soul. He knows that by committing sin he harms himself. In the words of the Archangel Raphael, "they that commit sin and iniquity are enemies of their own soul" (Tobit 12:10).

Some people think that the very fact of being a spirit makes sin impossible, and that to arrive at the spirit-state is to arrive at sinlessness. This, of course, is diametrically opposed to Catholic dogma. Sin is possible only with spiritual beings. The sin of Lucifer and his angels was all the greater because it was committed by pure spirits.

Mortal sin is essentially a disorder; it is a break in the universal harmony.

Man belongs to God, to mankind, and to himself. He sins because he puts himself in opposition to God or to mankind, or to himself.

Belonging to God, he owes to God duties of religion; they are the most necessary and the most sacred part of his moral life. He owes to God subjection of intellect and will. To neglect any of his duties towards Him, or to rebel with intellect or will, is a grievous disorder, because man has placed himself in opposition to the order and harmony of uncreated Good.

As a member of mankind, the individual has towards all his fellowmen duties of justice and charity. The violation of these duties puts him into opposition to the human order.

Finally, man is not a simple entity; he is a composition of spirit and matter; order and harmony in his personality are attained only when the body obeys the spirit.

If man were not a composite being, he could not sin against himself; there would be only the two other kinds of disorder for him; but being two in one, it will be disorder if the lower part of his being is not subject to the higher.

It is not unusual to hear people say: "As long as my act remains within myself, where is the sin? I have not hurt anyone."

This is a dangerous sophism. Man is bound more to himself than to mankind; he has to watch over the harmony between his own soul and body.

This personal harmony comes next after the harmony between the soul and God. Saint Thomas Aquinas teaches that suicide is a greater sin than murder. This is the reason why deliberate acts of unlawful self-indulgence are to be considered as grievous moral transgressions, though there may be no wrong done to anyone except the sinner himself.

Sin comes into the soul through free will. It is free will that makes or mars the soul. Now the will is an entirely spiritual power; there is nothing of sense-activity in it. Free will has a twofold way of entering into sin: by direct act and by consent.

The will does evil directly through itself; for instance, when there is the resolution of doing an injustice to one's neighbor, the will makes itself directly guilty. In sensual indulgence, the sinful act is done by the body, but as the will could prevent the sin, and does not, it sins by consent; thus the sensual indulgence becomes the sin of the spiritual soul.

The more there is of free will in a sinful act, the more there is of guilt; and sins done by the will direct are sins in a fuller measure than the sins committed by mere consent.

We come now to an aspect of sin which I might call Catholic, and which belongs to Catholic dogma. Mortal sin, of whatever category, is always a grievous injury done to God's Majesty, and this we say not only of sins committed directly against God, such as blasphemy, but also of sins which are not a direct violation of a duty to God, as for instance sins of impurity. The impure man, through his guilty indulgence, has offended God. Even if we had no rational explanation for this indirect result of sin, we should have to believe it through Faith. A sinful act can never be a merely philosophical disorder, without theological consequences. God is offended through every moral disorder of man. The atheist himself could not avoid offending God through his moral transgressions. Our masters give this explanation: God is infinite Good and Beauty, and as such has a strict right to be the object of every creature's aspirations, to be every creature's last end and eternal resting place. Through willful moral obliquity the sinner, as far as in him lies, makes himself unfit for the eternal Beauty, the eternal Good, and thus offends against the rights of that Beauty which is ever old and ever new.

It is, I think, clear from what has been said, that we make of the spiritual upheaval inside the soul the one disastrous result that makes sin so frightful.

We have all come across people whom we are justified in calling slaves of sin, men in whom repeated acts of sensual intemperance have produced evil habits, sinful cravings; their character has been radically ruined; their moral habits are irremediably warped. A common and frequent case is the drunkard. In him we see how the wages of sin is death, how the sinner bears the mark of his sin deep in his body.

Yet this is only a surface phenomenon. The sociologist is chiefly interested in this aspect of sin. The theologian sees deeper. For him, the disorder lies in the spirit itself. There is an irremediable opposition in that spirit to universal harmony. It is what is called in theology the stain of sin. It is a mortal wound, to be healed only by miraculous grace; its first result is to make the soul absolutely unfit for the possession of sanctifying grace and consequently of eternal life, of the vision of God.

The opposition of a soul in mortal sin to sanctifying grace is a necessary, unchanging opposition. This becomes evident if we consider that sanctifying grace is the created participation of God's uncreated beauty, while mortal sin establishes the soul in a state of moral hideousness.

We do not say that the loss of sanctifying grace is mortal sin. What we say is this: mortal sin is a moral decay of the soul incompatible with sanctifying grace. The first mortal sin committed by a man banishes from his soul all the graces it had received, even if they had been high enough to make him into a seraph. Subsequent mortal sins have the same evil effects as the first. Generally the evil of the second is greater than the evil of the first; for though no sanctifying grace is driven out of the soul by the second sin, the spirit is corrupted more profoundly, the sinner makes himself more unfit for the return of grace and puts himself into a state of opposition to universal harmony that will make his loss to be death within death. For we believe that the main suffering of the lost soul in eternal reprobation is the direct and necessary result of the willful disorderly act. The greater the will's distortion, the keener the realization of the loss, of utter disorderliness.

We must remember, however, that this corruption of the spirit of which we are speaking here is not to be understood as a weakening of mental power, as a blunting of the edge of will and intellect, so that a time might come when, through the accumulation of sins, the spiritual powers of the soul should have reached a minimum of activity.

This does take place sometimes in the body when senses commit sin. But the spirit never loses its vividness and energy; its corruption therefore must be understood in the sense of an accumulation of positive acts, of oppositions to the harmony of the universe. The will is getting, as it were, stronger and bolder to carry the burden of its iniquity.

An instance from life might serve here. A man who once entangles himself in unfair business transactions never loses any of his shrewdness or his callousness through going deeper and deeper into felony and malpractice. In fact, the small roguery prepares him for the big one, till he finds himself hopelessly in opposition to the rights of the society in which he lives.

So with the accumulation of entirely spiritual transgressions: their repetition, far from weakening the spirit, establishes it in a more resolute opposition to eternal harmony.

These are the most important points to be remembered concerning the enemy of our soul. We do not wonder, therefore, that the saint has such a horror of sin, as he feels keenly the beauty and greatness of the soul, and as he knows that nothing but the soul's own act can be a danger, or a poison, to it.

Chapter 22

Venial Sin

Catholic theology is not only clear in its views on the nature and result of sin, it is also wise and prudent in distinguishing between sin and sin. If there is mortal sin, there is also venial sin; and with the courage that makes Catholic theology pronounce mortal sin to be the evil of the soul, is united the wisdom that makes it declare venial sin to be no loss of God.

In fact venial sin is not sin on a small scale, while mortal sin is sin on a large scale; venial sin is to mortal sin what a wound in a strong and healthy body is to a corpse. The fair comparison is not between a big wound and a small wound; but venial sin is like a curable wound in a living body, while mortal sin is death.

Nowhere do we find that gift of prudence, which is the special gift of Catholic theology, come out more strongly than in this doctrine of venial sin. The Pharisee might take scandal at some of the conclusions of theology.

Sin is venial for two reasons: first, on account of the incompleteness of the human act; secondly, on account of the transgression being merely of secondary laws.

Speaking of mortal sin we said that all its guilt comes from the fact of the will freely choosing it. Now we may easily conceive, and the study of human nature gives us many practical instances, how human passion may reach a disproportionate violence; the control of the will over the emotion is no longer complete; the predominance of sensual appetite is such as to overwhelm the will. In a case like this, what would have been mortal sin becomes venial sin, on account of the will's imperfect control.

Mortal sin requires that free will be not impeded in its action through any preponderance of the lower appetites. The attraction of sensuality must not be more than an allurement to the will, if the will's freedom is to be preserved.

It is often, of course, very difficult, in individual cases, to decide whether or not the lower appetites leave the spiritual will enough freedom to assert its control; it is the secret of God who searches the heart and the reins. But theology asserts the universal principle that may at least make us cautious in judging our brother, as we do not know the working of his soul. In practice, too, it is better to admit to ourselves the full guilt of our deed, and not flatter ourselves that perhaps we were not quite responsible for the act that makes us blush.

But by far the greater number of venial sins come from the nature of the precept transgressed. There are transgressions of the universal laws that are the destruction of the moral order and moral harmony: they make sin mortal. But then there are transgressions which are no such destruction. To speak a deliberate falsehood in a matter that will not involve grievous wrong to a neighbor will only be a venial sin, because it is considered that such a transgression is not a destruction of the universal order. We assume here that the sin is committed with clear knowledge and full freedom; but this circumstance alone does not make it into a mortal sin. Through a deliberate falsehood, without injury to the neighbor, no vital law of the universe has been violated. Deliberation, as such, does not make a transgression mortal, as many people suppose, when, on the other hand, there is no vital law violated. In such case the sin remains venial.

It would be very difficult for human reason to define which of the laws of the moral order are vital or non-vital. The most learned of men have erred greatly in apportioning to the various aberrations of the human heart their proper measure of guilt. This incapability of accurately determining the relative importance of the elements that make up the moral order is one of the facts that postulate a divine Authority to guide man. With the utterances of the sacred Scriptures and the definitions of the Church, we Catholics are fully instructed in this most burning question. There is not one species of moral transgression which, considered objectively, has not been labelled by Catholic theology as either mortal or venial. This gives great peace to the Christian conscience, and prevents pharisaical pruderies.

One of the doctrines insisted upon by our masters is this: venial sin does not diminish sanctifying grace, does not reduce the measure of divine charity that is found in the soul. Venial sin has no power on the higher parts of the human soul. Just as there may be differences among friends that are not the death of friendship, so likewise there may be differences where God and the soul are concerned that leave the divine life in the soul. This is a favorite simile with theologians when treating of the result of venial sin. They say that venial sin is no diminution of the sanctifying grace that is in the soul. For all along, even in the most deliberate act of venial sin, man has his ultimate aspirations fixed on God. He knows that the act of moral imperfection he is committing does not ruin his soul, and therefore does not make him incapable of possessing the divine Good.

Saint Thomas frequently says that venial sin is not against grace, but outside grace; he even goes so far as to say that grace is the master of the human will in the very act of committing venial sin. This is to be understood to mean that sanctifying grace and charity so control the human will that yields to venial sin, that the act would not be committed by the will if it were a mortal sin.

So far we have considered venial sin from what I might call its relative aspect, comparing it with mortal sin. Mortal sin is the greatest of evils, so we need not be surprised to find the sin that is not mortal judged so much more leniently.

But nothing would be less Catholic than to speak or think of venial sin lightly. It is a great evil, but an evil that is compatible with the privileges of the children of God. In all this I am speaking of a soul in a state of sanctifying grace as committing venial sin. We know that a man in a state of mortal sin may commit venial sin, as well as the man in a state of grace; in that case venial sin is chiefly a hindrance to the sinner's return to God, and conversion will be more difficult.

Venial sins are disobedience to the laws of God, and are punished as such by temporary and finite sanctions. To make full amends for them would not require a Divine Redeemer, as mortal sin does; the soul that has committed venial sin may make full amends, if it be in the state of grace.

Another axiom of which theologians are fond is this: no accumulation of venial sins will ever make one mortal sin.

On the other hand, the chief mischief of venial sin lies in its fatal power to pave the way to mortal sin. This, of course, must be understood only of the fully deliberate venial sin. It is an obvious psychological law that repeated venial sin, committed with all due deliberation, must of necessity lessen in the soul the horror for sin and evil generally. It must deprive it of that delicacy of conscience which is the soul's greatest protection. The removal of this safeguard makes the soul an easy prey to serious moral temptation.

There is only one more remark to make with regard to the soul's relation to sin. Venial sin can only be a human phenomenon, not an angelic one; nay, more, it is a phenomenon of this life only. The angel and the disembodied soul cannot sin venially. The reason of this is to be found in that kind of divisibility which our mental operations have in this life. Now we can do things by halves, and while one part of the moral man may be deflected, the main portion of him may still be sound and whole. No such divisibility is possible for a spirit, who does whatever he undertakes with the totality of his powers.

Chapter 23

The Soul's Responsibility

A sin is essentially the act of the will, I intend in this chapter to say more on the soul's share in the commission of sin, and its responsibility for that act. It is not my intention, however, to discuss human responsibility from the point of view of freedom, or liberty; I take human freedom for granted. I regard the soul's responsibility from the point of view of diversity of powers and faculties in the human individual. The question is this: which of man's faculties is answerable for the deeds done in the body, since multiplicity of faculties or powers is the most striking feature in man's individuality?

Broadly speaking, we may distinguish in man two regions: the animal and the spirit. This division is based on the primordial fact of man being a compound of a spiritual soul and a material body. Catholic philosophy never spiritualized the body, and never materialized the soul.

But this broad distinction into two regions has to be stated with qualification. As soul and body form one person, the two must be united in some way. The soul, from its spirit-nature, being the main factor, could not be said to be united to the body unless it be through a direct act of beneficent influence on the body, as I have already shown. Here then we have a third factor of great importance. In man there is that part which comes from the fact of animal senses being raised, through the presence of a spiritual substance, to a much higher level of activity and potentiality, and acquiring through it a new power no animal could ever possess. It is a most important element in the Catholic philosophy of man. These new faculties could not be spirit-faculties. They are essentially sense-faculties, but sense-faculties of an exceedingly high order, of wonderful resourcefulness. Our masters give them a generic name; they call them *Cogitativa*. They ascribe to them a wonderfully wide range of psychological activity; and things which the uninitiated might put down to the pure spirit-intellect in man, our philosophers still consider to be within the scope of *Cogitativa*.

So the hierarchy would be this: on the summit there is the spirit-intellect, with the corresponding spirit-will where there is freedom of choice. Then there is this wonderful *Cogitativa*, with its corresponding appetites, which we cannot call "will," because "will" is reserved to the spirit's free choice, though we are perfectly safe in calling it a "lower will." It is the region of sense, but the highest, purest region among the senses. The noblest and greatest results of the soul's influence on the body are there. Then come the powers and activities and appetites which we share with other animals and which the physical sciences and medical skill have taken for their province.

The second region, *Cogitativa*, is of greater interest than any other in the psychology of man. It is there where education, heredity, environment, do so much. The theologian who, to my mind, gives *Cogitativa* its fullest importance, is the great disciple of Saint Thomas, Cajetan; he even gives it an initial and imperfect reflective free will tendency. But in this he only follows his great master Aquinas.

I cannot enter into all the psychological considerations and critical observations the subject suggests; enough for me to say here that our masters give to the senses of man as much as any modern materialist ever did. They are wise materialists; they differ from the modern materialist, not because they reduce the role of sense-life in man in favor of a problematic spirit-life, but because they assert that in man's life there are phenomena which are absolutely beyond the senses, beyond even that higher region called *Cogitativa*. Their position is unassailable, as they give a purely spirit explanation for phenomena for which the materialist has no explanation at all, and for which he can have no explanation. Our masters compare *Cogitativa* with the instincts of some clever animal. But this is only a comparison. They give *Cogitativa* a much higher range than mere animal instinct. Instinct enables the animal to judge in certain particular things that belong to the preservation of its life. So *Cogitativa* is a faculty of judging in all things in which there enter no universals. We see at a glance what a wide range this gives to *Cogitativa*, and how many of our deeds depend upon its activities.

But to come to responsibility; how far are we accountable for the acts of *Cogitativa*? I take *Cogitativa* here, both as a knowing and a willing power. Cajetan gives *Cogitativa*, quite independently of the intellectual soul, enough free will for venial sin; mortal sin there could never be there, because it is only the region of the senses, though it be the summit of them.

Most of the sinful impulses in man have in *Cogitativa* not only their origin, but also their battlefield. It is the region of our emotions. If sin is delight and pleasure taken in evil, it is *Cogitativa* that has the pleasure, that is delighted. It is what our masters express when they say that our senses, or at least our higher senses, are *subiectum peccati*, the region where sin takes place.

How then is it possible that any of the transgressions or disorders that happen on this plane should be mortal transgressions, should be grievous sins, entailing the loss of sanctifying grace, that wonderful gift, which abides not in the summit of the senses, but in the summit of the spirit? The spirit-will, our masters say, gives its consent, and by giving that consent to *Cogitativa*, it has made itself guilty of the grievous transgression, not because it transgressed grievously itself, but because it did not prevent the transgression when it could. The spirit, of course, or rather the spirit-will, has its own transgressions, its own disorders; such, for instance, would be the act of the man who willingly and deliberately schemes the financial ruin of his neighbor; such again is the act of the proud mind, unwilling to submit to higher authority, from sheer pride. But what we mean to emphasize here is this, that even the highest senses cannot be said to be entirely responsible for their acts to the tribunal of morality. The immaterial spirit-will must come in, at least as the consenting party.

These considerations have another advantage: they may help us to establish what I may call the hierarchy of guilt. Nothing could be more profitable to the men of our generation than a clear and certain gradation of moral depravities. Our fellow countrymen, unfortunately, are ill instructed in the appreciation of moral guilt; people seem more and more to judge the gravity of sin from social results.

The greatest moral depravity is to be found in intellectual sins, rebellions of the mind against revealed divine truth and established authority. Next come the sins against justice. These two classes of sins are the exclusive acts of the spirit-will of man. Then, and only then, come the sins that might be called generically sins against morality. As far as these sins do not imply a violation of duty to our neighbor or society, by giving scandal or by doing harm otherwise, they make man less guilty before God, though they may make him more contemptible in the eyes of the world.

CHAPTER 24

Distinction between Vice and Sin

The foregoing chapter has prepared us for a distinction that should help us to judge our neighbor more fairly, and on that account I work it out more fully here.

Catholic philosophy may be said to be an extremely charitable philosophy, if we take charity here for a kindly interpretation of our neighbor's deeds. It judges no man, though it be so uncompromising about the claims of truth and justice, though it never calls good evil or evil good. It clearly distinguishes between virtue and vice, moral order and moral disorder, but never says of any man that he has offended God.

Catholic moral theology makes free will, and free will alone the region where there can be sin. Its tendency is to restrict the limits of that sphere of our soul where there can be sin, rather than to extend them. It never considers as sin any depravity which man cannot help committing. Through ability to distinguish the essential qualities of a human act the Catholic view of sin has become the most rational view.

There is one distinction amongst all others which deserves our attention here. It is the distinction between vice and sin, or that responsibility for evil which we call guilt. "Vice," that most harsh of English terms, stands in philosophy for any confirmed habit of mind and body which becomes an endless source of moral short-comings.

Vice being generally a habit of easy observation, we know when a man has it, and we know too when he gives way to it; we cannot, and need not, shut our eyes to the fact.

We have all known men who are the slaves of intemperance. Even Charity has open eyes, and does not bid us to doubt the existence of obvious shortcomings. The same with mental or intellectual inferiorities; we need to coerce ourselves into a belief that so and so is a wise, prudent and thoughtful man, when everybody speaks of the rashness and foolishness of his deeds. In fact we are often strictly bound to take into account our neighbor's caliber, to have a low opinion, say, of his prudence; we have to avoid putting our trust in his judgment. Scripture frequently cautions us against the fool. There is the gift of discernment of spirits, that helps us to distinguish the capable and reliable from the incapable and unreliable. But at the same time we are never authorized to judge his guilt, we are never justified in pronouncing finally against our brother, still less in talking about it to everybody.

Vice may be in a man, and frequently is in a man, not through his own act. If it were known of any individual that his depraved habits are the results of repeated free acts, it would be certain in his case that, in the past, he had offended God, because the acts were free. But the evil habit once acquired, though it be through free acts, is no longer a free disposition, and I am never in a position to say that he is a sinner, because he has evil propensities.

The offense against God is the free determination of the will to select the forbidden pleasure. When is it that such a free determination takes place in the breast of a man? I do not know: God alone knows. I may know a certain man to be a hopeless case of disorderliness, rashness and imprudence; but I can never say that he is a sinner, because I have no means of watching the acts of his free will. Those moral shortcomings, called vicious habits, far from giving us the measure of a man's guilt, ought to have the opposite effect, as it is in their nature to curtail his freedom of action and choice. The eye of God must often see an upright will under all the mental eccentricities and ethical infirmities that cover some unfortunate human being, as with a cloak of malediction.

The opposite proposition too, no doubt, finds its application, where, with a cool head and most respectable character, there may be rebellion against God, which is the greatest of all sins.

In practice, in our human relations, we have to know from what shortcomings many people suffer, as our lives are bound up with theirs; but this is all we need know. Whether they are sinners in the eyes of God is not of any earthly concern, and to my mind this distinction between vice and guilt is one that will make us very patient with the moral infirmities of our brothers.

Chapter 25

Original Sin and the Human Soul

The theology of the human soul would indeed be most incomplete without an exposition of the doctrine of original sin. Original sin is the first chapter in the history of the human

The unpopularity of this old Christian dogma with the modern mind could hardly be an excuse for omitting to state it here. I feel confident, in fact, that nothing can reconcile the thoughtful mind with original sin except an exact and technical exposition of it such as we find in the writings of theologians. Nothing shows more clearly what a high opinion our masters had of the spirituality of the human soul than their teaching on original sin.

The one consideration that is of paramount importance in this matter is this: all the evils and all the harm done to the human soul through the fall of man, and through original sin, are evils by comparison with a higher good. Original sin cannot be described in itself; it has to be stated by comparison, and the term of comparison is the high and privileged state in which man was originally created; we must keep our eyes fixed on that ideal state if we are to understand original sin.

The temptation to make original sin consist in the woes and limitations of human nature is obvious. Yet our masters never yielded to it; they always looked for the stain of original sin in that region of the soul which is accessible to God alone. I feel confident that I am not exaggerating when I affirm that original sin presupposes such an idea of God and of the human soul as is not found outside the Catholic Church. To deny the existence of original sin, on scientific or humanitarian grounds, is an unwarranted intrusion into the sanctuary of theology on the part of experimental science.

It is characteristic of Catholic theology that, while lifting the spiritual facts far above the region of sentimentality and imagination, far above the working of the senses, it still safeguards their intense reality. This is especially true in the case of original sin. It is a great evil, an evil forever to be bewailed, yet flesh and blood have little to do with it.

The reason why some find it so difficult to give original sin its proper place in their philosophy of the human soul is this: they do not grasp how the most important sphere of the soul's life is for God directly and exclusively, and original sin has to be sought for in this high region where God and the soul meet.

When God created man, He put into his soul a gift technically called the gift of original justice. By means of that gift, whose psychological and supernatural value cannot be overestimated, the human will was made perfect. The human will, through that gift, and as long as the gift was in the soul, was adjusted in such wise that God Himself could not discover anything in it that was not worthy of Him. Now it is the loss of that extraordinary gift that constitutes original sin. All other losses do not constitute original sin; they are mere results of original sin; even if they had not been inflicted on the soul, there would still be original sin. On the other hand, all these deficiencies may be in the soul, and yet original sin be removed through the restoration of that wonderful gift. Such is the case of the baptized soul in the state of grace.

That gift of original justice, for such is its technical name, whatever it was, made the human will perfectly subordinate to the will of God, established it in perfect harmony with God; the loss of it brought about a falling back of the soul upon itself, which need not be a positive rebellion against God, yet which, by comparison with that first adhesion of the will to God, looks like rebellion. (We must remember what we said at the beginning, that in the study of original sin we have to go by comparisons.)

The human soul now begins its career without this gift, and this is original sin. It is a privation, because God meant the soul to have this gift. It is a state of enmity to God, again by comparison, because without this gift the human will cannot rise above itself with an unselfish preference for God. The absence of this gift is rightly called a sin, because the loss is a consequence of the free act of a human will, the will of Adam. That Saint Thomas should call the absence of that gift from the individual soul the formal element of original sin is a clear evidence of his immaterialistic view of the doctrine. The term "formal," with the Schoolmen, is what we might call in English the essential, the decisive part. It is certainly a remarkable fact that Saint Thomas and his disciples should have given to original sin that exclusive meaning, apparently so abstruse and so lofty, when the belief in original sin fills the writings of the Fathers with an unceasing lament. It may be admitted, of course, that the Fathers do not always distinguish between original sin and the fallen state, yet the distinction is of paramount importance.

Death of the body, the flesh that wars against the spirit and the spirit that wars against the flesh, the infirmity of will and ignorance of mind that make temptation so dangerous, all that dismal condition of human nature bewailed so eloquently by Saint Paul and Saint Augustine, are not original sin. They constitute the Fall. Baptism, which destroys original sin, does not alter those sad conditions of our nature.

The question might be asked here: how can the human soul possibly be said to be in a state of even comparative opposition to God, through the lack of the gift of original justice? The soul comes direct from the hands of God as a pure spirit. Why then should it be considered less directly turned towards God simply because it lacks that higher direction that comes through the gift of original justice?

The answer is to be found in our chapter on the soul's unconsciousness, where we said that in the present union between soul and body the soul's activities are taken up entirely in animating the body. It is, through the laws of its nature, such a "pouring out" of the soul over matter (such is the expression of Saint Thomas), that brings comparative inability to rise to God directly, totally, with all its strength; and it was the office of the gift of original justice to remedy that inevitable immersion of the spirit in matter.

Here we come, by a natural sequence, to the mode of transmission of original sin. It took a long time before theology could state clearly, without any materialist appendages, how the sin of Adam is transmitted to all the human race. To make of natural heredity the bearer of the original stain was found to be one of the theological exaggerations. Heredity in fact, as Saint Thomas points out so shrewdly, far from causing a moral stain, does away with it, because whatever comes through heredity does not belong to the moral order, but to the physical order.

What we need to explain in original sin is the depravity, at least comparative, of the spirit-will in man; for there alone could be the stain of sin. But the spirit part of man does not fall under heredity. The mode of transmission then which alone is recognized by Saint Thomas and Catholic theologians generally is simply the fact of one human being coming from another human being through the laws of generation, or, more simply, the fact of our being the children, through successive generations, of Adam. In this matter of original sin, what might be called the concupiscent character of the act of propagation need not be considered at all. A child would have original sin even if his parents, by an impossible fiction, were entirely exempt from the laws of concupiscence. This supposition comes from Saint Thomas himself. The union between the spirit that comes from the hands of God, the soul, and the human organism that comes from the parents, is the only physical cause that makes original sin.

We ought not to expect to find in that human organism a kind of spiritual virus that will poison the soul. The gift that was to be the compensating power between the two elements, soul and body, is not given when the union takes place, solely because it has been forfeited by the race through the act of the father of mankind.

Of course, in the writings of the Fathers and other preachers, we come across many strong expressions that suggest a kind of spiritual infection, a deadly spiritual poison that kills the soul when it is united with the body. Although their language is metaphorical, it is hardly exaggerated; for the soul to be without the gift that would raise it above the body is indeed a great loss. A gift of that kind cannot but be a gratuitous bestowal, yet at the same time one which, from its extreme usefulness, might almost be called one of nature's necessities. The lamentations of the preacher over the sad condition of the unregenerate soul are as fully justified as most other complaints of the children of men, with whom misfortune is mostly such by comparison. They are not as happy as they have been, or would like to be, and therefore they are most unhappy.

Perhaps some of my readers will detect a difficulty in the exposition of these views, the discovery of which would do credit to their theological insight. Original sin, we have said, is that most spirit-like disorder of the will which is remedied at baptism through sanctifying grace, in fact original sin is entirely destroyed through sanctifying grace in whatever way it comes. Now sanctifying grace may be lost again, as we all know. Does then original sin come back?

Original sin does not come back, and this for two reasons. First, if God gives sanctifying grace to the human soul, through that very act He has severed the soul from that solidarity which made it share the condition of fallen mankind. Sanctifying grace, possessed even once, has raised the soul to the family of God. If the soul loses it again, it is a rebellious member in the family of God, but does not fall back into a merely common membership with the human family.

In the second place, original sin, from all that has preceded, is evidently a state which, as far as the individual is concerned, is not of his own doing. Not to be of his doing is an essential feature in it. But when a man loses sanctifying grace he loses it through his own doing, and his state is not original sin, but actual mortal sin, which of course is infinitely more disastrous for him individually.

What is the precise relation to original sin of all those active disorders in the human faculties called concupiscence? We have seen how they remain, when original sin has been taken away.

Saint Thomas calls them the material part of original sin, while that higher spiritual deprivation is the formal part. In Scholastic language material is to formal as a kind of result, a secondary consequence, of indifferent moral value. In themselves our concupiscences are not sin, they are not a moral depravity, they are mere infirmities. They are wounds, not indeed of the soul, but of the body. They are called in theology the wounds of human nature. Cajetan has a wise remark. He says that we know them to be wounds, not through observation, but through faith. His meaning is this, that a being such as man, from his very nature, is prone to the things that are not of the spirit; and moreover he must die by the laws of his nature. There was once in man a state of gratuitous psychological perfection through which those natural necessities were suspended. It is entirely a matter of faith that man's estate was at any time so high that a falling away from it is tantamount to being stripped and wounded. Once more, the wounding, as everything else in original sin, is to be taken comparatively. There is a declaration of the Holy Office that it is erroneous for a theologian to maintain that God would have been unjust in creating man in the condition in which he now finds himself.

A final remark I think it well to make before ending has reference to the well-known power of the evil spirit over the unregenerate soul. It must be a great reality; we need only follow the ritual of Baptism to find there the casting out of the devil holding a conspicuous place. This evil presence founded on original sin seems to be in conflict with the main idea of this thesis, that everything in original sin is to be understood comparatively. The power of the evil spirit over the unregencrated soul seems to be an absolute evil, not only a comparative one. This evil presence, however, does not seem to belong to original sin, but to the fallen state. Just as what we called the material part of original sin, so perhaps, more than anything else, Satan's principality over the earth was established through the personal act of Adam. That the spirit of rebellion had taken up his abode on the earth before the Fall is evident from the Scriptures. The supernatural, or, in other words, sanctifying grace, is the only barrier that could possibly be opposed to him; and the absence, either willful or inborn, of the supernatural makes a presence of the evil spirit at least possible.

CHAPTER 26

Original Sin and the Fall of Man

On the subject of man's present condition we have to proceed cautiously, in order to avoid compromising sacred doctrine. There is at the outset a most important distinction to be drawn between original sin and the fallen state. The importance of this distinction will appear after a moment's consideration.

Original sin is wiped away in Baptism, yet after Baptism, as before, we are still a fallen race. The Fall is remedied, not in this life, but in the resurrection of all flesh. Original sin, on the contrary, is entirely destroyed through the possession of sanctifying grace.

Again, the present state of mankind shows endless varieties of decadence and retrogression, which may all be traced back to an historical origin. Science and observation can explain them without any theology. Thus the dwarfishness in the inhabitant of the Arctic regions can easily be explained climatically. It would be most unwise of a theologian to appeal to the various instances of degeneracy we notice in mankind for evidence in support of the dogma of the primeval Fall. Those retrogressions are processes of history; they establish indeed the fact that we are an imperfect race, but they can never establish the theological doctrine of the original Fall.

Mankind might be a thousand times more perfect than it is; in fact, all the *Utopias* of the idealistic dreamer about the perfectibility of mankind might be fulfilled, and yet the Fall of which theology speaks would be as great and as real as ever.

Endless perfectibility of mankind is not a theory at which a theologian need look askance. No degree of perfection realized in practice is a healing of that wound which is our fall in Adam.

We may, if we like, think of our first parents, after they left the garden of innocence and delight, as of beings full of every perfection. Quite likely their existence was actually more ideal than the Golden Age of the poets. Instances of degeneracy in the past, and hopes of future perfection, are alike foreign to the dogma of the Fall. We may hold them on their own merits.

The fall of Adam and for that matter our own fallen state, within the limits defined by theology, is a thing no one can deny on scientific grounds, because the Fall is the loss of a state entirely supernatural, entirely gratuitous, entirely miraculous. The moment there is a possibility in the human breast of feeling the stings of an evil inclination, man, according to theology, is a fallen being. Even if the evil inclination were not followed by consent, it would still be a clear indication of the Fall. The perfection of Adam was this, not to be able to have any discrepancies in mind or heart between eternal truth, eternal beauty, and his own desires. To begin to feel those disharmonies is already deepest fall. Theology and faith do not go beyond this. This is the Fall they know; and if man has fallen lower still, it is the historian's part to explain it and to bewail it.

We might say indeed that all the evils of the world are the result of Adam's fall; but they are not *the* Fall. The Fall would have been just as real even if by a special intervention of divine Providence those results had not taken place.

Neither biology, evolution, nor even psychology, can be pressed into service by the theologian to prove his dogma, just as they cannot speak against it. For the biologist to denounce the dogmatic fact of the Fall is to go beyond his competence. Original sin, if possible, dwells in a region still more inaccessible to science and observation. It is, as Saint Thomas says, the *supremum hominis*, the highest part of man, and that alone, which is the seat of original sin.

I think I may safely assert that most non-Catholics would hardly grant the possibility of such supernatural elevation of human nature as is implied in original sin. For original justice means this, that by a special dispensation of God, by a miracle hardly less astounding than transubstantiation, every human being who receives life from another human being should receive it in such a way as to be radically and intrinsically fit for the blessed Vision of God; that the mysteries of human generation, already so great, should have been rendered still more mysterious through man having eternal life and sanctifying grace through natural heredity. For such would have been the condition of mankind without original sin.

Sanctifying grace was to be, in the happy phrase of Saint Thomas, the grace of the race, instead of its being the grace of only particular individuals. We must bear in mind that original sin, contrary to the teaching of the Reformers, leaves man all his powers to acquire special grace, through his own personal acts, under the influence of the Holy Spirit. All that the dogma of the Fall prohibits us from saying is this, that man inherits grace from his parents. The original privilege was this: to be conceived and born with such grace as to make the soul radically fit for the Vision of God. Where then is the injustice? Where is man's right to grumble at the ways of God? Had we been denied the power of finding grace through our own acts, we might perhaps have had reason to think God rigorous in His ways. Catholic theology is emphatic in leaving those powers to man, though of course those same powers have to be helped by the grace of God.

In this matter, only those have a right to speak of the severity of the ways of God who are firm believers in the generosity of God's original plan.

In conclusion, it is not so much original sin and the Fall that are difficulties; it is the state of original justice and perfection that would seem fabulous,, if we had not faith. To be, through the laws of heredity, immortal in body, divine in soul, without error in the mind, without defect or imperfection of any kind; such was God's first intention for man.

CHAPTER 27

The Human Soul and Suffering

Suffering is the daily bread of man here on earth. Possible suffering in the hereafter constitutes one of the most vexing, as well as one of the most dreadful, problems for man's mind. It is the purpose of the present chapter to give the theological teaching as to the extent and the manner in which the soul, as such, partakes of suffering.

In this matter we have to distinguish between the two states of the human soul: the state of union with the body and its disembodied state; for the soul's position with regard to suffering is exactly reversed, as either the one or the other state prevails.

It must be taken as a universal truth that there is no suffering, in the real sense of the word, for the human soul, as long as it is united with the body. For the soul to suffer now, while it animates the body, would be as great a miracle as if the soul had direct and experimental knowledge of its own existence. I do not deny the possibility of such a miracle; perhaps soul-sufferings, properly so called, do occasionally take place in the lives of some of the great mystics, though it would be a difficult task to bring forward sufficient evidence of this from their own disclosures of the secrets of their hearts. Even the mental agonies more bitter than death of which there are a few authentic instances, may be explained without having recourse to direct soul-sufferings.

Soul-sufferings, as the term implies, are sufferings in which the human spirit suffers directly as spirit, in itself, in one of his purely spiritual powers. Such sufferings do not take place here on earth. All our sufferings are either bodily pains, or sorrows that have their seat in the higher senses. Even when we are thwarted in the most spirit-like part of ourselves, in our free will, the consequent annoyance is felt, not in the will, but in a lower faculty, the sensitive part of our being. The spirit-will of man either acts, or ceases to act, but it cannot suffer.

Catholic theologians have rendered us a great service by showing how suffering does not reach what is man's noblest and serenest region, his real spirit-faculties. Catholic theology is a most sympathetic theology, because it believes fully in the objective reality of suffering; it never treats suffering as an illusion; on the contrary, it makes it one of the most powerful levers for sanctity, as there is such intense reality in suffering. On the other hand, Catholic theology is not overwhelmed by the terrible phenomena of suffering. It views them as the clouds that cling to the sides of a mountain; the real summit of the human personality soars above them.

Saint Thomas Aquinas gives this matter of the soul's sufferings and emotions the attention and the prominence it deserves, in the Twenty-sixth Question of his treatise *De Veritate*. Nothing could surpass the lucidity of his views on the subject, coupled as they are with a most profound analysis of the sources of suffering. He speaks of the sense of pain very much like a modern psychologist; he makes the highest appetitive senses the chief, and in fact the only, organs of soul-sufferings. Soul-sufferings, *passiones animales*, are, in the language of Saint Thomas, those depressing and painful states of the higher appetitive senses that come from the intellectual perception of an unpleasant thing. Thus, for instance, I may be thwarted in a cherished scheme; my mind and my free will perceive this check put upon my activities. But mind and will are not the sufferers; the sadness will be in the highest appetitive power of the sensitive part of my being. This is the nearest approach to real soul-suffering; in this instance, an intellectual act, or disposition, establishes the appetitive power of the higher senses in a state of sadness. In this sense only may we say that our souls suffer.

Even the greatest sufferings, such as Christ's agony in the garden, are to be explained in that way. No intellectual act, no volitional act, of the purely spiritual order can be suffering, though it may be an apprehension of what is most unpleasant. The sensitive powers that come just below experience all the suffering. Pain and sorrow belong to our sensitive, organic powers; pain and sorrow may be the results of purely intellectual, purely immaterial considerations and dispositions, but they are results which are not inside, but outside the immaterial, the intellectual region itself. A pure spirit is as superior to pain and sorrow as it is to sensation; in other words, pain and sorrow are against the laws of spirit-life.

Such statements will surprise, at first sight, when we remember our belief in Hell and Purgatory. Yet the views expressed here are no more than the logical conclusions of the doctrine on the nature of spirit-substances; hence they are the constant teaching of Saint Thomas Aquinas. My chapter on spirit-penalty will, I hope, set at rest any alarm an orthodox mind might experience at these conclusions of Scholastic philosophy. For the present, anyone with a logical mind will see at a glance the reasonableness, as well as the wisdom of the Scholastic view on pain and sorrow which makes them into exclusively bodily phenomena.

There is a way, however, in which Saint Thomas would grant that the soul, as such, suffers: it only needs a passing mention, as it confirms all we have said. Bodily suffering interferes with the higher operations of the soul, it may even bring about the separation of soul and body, which separation, as we have said elsewhere, is a loss to the soul. Illness, for instance, hampers purely intellectual speculation; pain distracts the most powerful mind from the contemplation of higher things. Such conditions, however, could not be called sufferings in the soul, or of the soul. They are merely negative results, consisting in transitory suspensions of certain soul-activities, in conformity with principles laid down elsewhere, principles according to which purely intellectual operations cannot be performed without the cooperation of sensitive organs.

Chapter 28

The Law of God and the Laws of Nature

We have now reached a stage in the treatment of our subject which needs constant reference to the concept of law, both in the physical and in the moral order. It will not be out of place therefore to say a few words about the laws of God and the universe.

We read a great deal in the sacred Scriptures about the ways of God. In this connection we may also speak of the character of God. Character is an unchanging feature even with man. It comes out everywhere, showing itself in the smallest details as well as in the greatest undertakings of life. Character is a man's way of acting. So with God, there is a way of acting that is characteristic of Him, and as far as our observation of divine Providence goes, we never discover a departure from that way.

The things of which we can say with absolute certainty that they are acts of God are first and foremost the great laws of Nature. Through reason and faith we know those marvels to be the direct effect of God's creative power, and immediately under His control. They are not only the invention of His infinite wisdom, the effects of His omnipotence, but they are also the product of His free choice. For who would dare to say that He could not have made Nature different from what it is? I do not maintain for a moment that there is no such thing as an inherent property, in the things of Nature, belonging to the very idea, the very essence of it, as the Schoolmen would say. Matter, for instance, seems hardly conceivable without the three dimensions; even God could not think of matter without reference to the three dimensions. But where the free act of God comes in is in the arranging, the combining, the coordination and subordination of the things which His wisdom has conceived, so as to make a world of His own choice. With the same materials, He could have made a different world. That the universe, as it now is, bears the marks not only of an intelligent cause, but also a free cause, is a matter of Catholic faith. And here we see the role of character in God. Being free in the arranging, in the planning of the physical world, He has invariably adopted one mode, one way, one style: permanence and unchangeableness.

Modern science has done theology a very great service in demonstrating these characteristics in all the works of God. Indeed, with modern science, the stability of Nature's laws has become almost a fetish. It perhaps too readily makes them into a kind of self-subsisting power that rules the universe with an iron hand. The laws of Nature are the gods, the demiurges of modern science. It fails to see God in Nature, precisely because the laws of Nature seem to account for everything. Yet those very laws are the will of God, and are moreover a clear expression of the Legislator's character. Nature resembles its Maker. Faint though the resemblance may be, it is a true one.

The same characteristics are found in another order of things, in the moral order, both in its individual and in its social aspects. To be under the law is to be benefited by it; to be outside the law is to be deprived of its blessings; to be in opposition to the law is to forfeit happiness. As sin is a disordered act, it is evident that whosoever sins acts against some kind of law; and therefore it is but fair that he should be thwarted by that very order, which thwarting is pain indeed.

Firm belief in the operation of laws, both in the physical and spiritual order, is compatible in the mind of the theologian with his belief in prayer; for prayer, far from interfering with laws, is one of the great laws of the human soul. Through prayer the human soul rises to a height of spiritual perfection which it could not attain otherwise. By prayer I mean here the prayer of supplication, the cry to God, that He in His Omnipotence may do what it is not possible for human nature to do. Such an attitude on the part of man is a moral perfection second to none in its excellency; through it the human will is made to trust God, a most difficult thing for a created spirit to do on account of the distance that separates him from God. Not to pray is not to observe a divine law, because God's law is that certain things should not be granted except in answer to prayer.

The role of prayer has puzzled many a mind. Most modern explanations of prayer, outside the sphere of Catholic thought, are tainted with pantheism; prayer is considered as an effort of the partially divine to unite with the wholly divine. Christian prayer, on the contrary, supposes all along two extremes, infinitely distant from each other: God and the creature. When prayer is heard the infinitely rich has not assimilated the poor suppliant; but He has made him less poor, perhaps He has even made him rich. But if we cannot understand what it is to trust God, our efforts to explain prayer will land us sooner or later in pantheistic theories. Trust, even absolute and unlimited trust, implies a duality of persons. It is a difficult virtue among men, and it is not less difficult between man and God. But where it is found, there is a union far more refreshing than the assimilation dreamed of by the pantheist. This is why I said that prayer is one of the great laws of the human soul; nothing else can take its place in the soul, and the soul without prayer is outside one of the loveliest regions of moral perfection, the sphere where human trust and divine liberality meet.

CHAPTER 29

Permanence of the Spirit-Will

Catholic theology is the theology of the laws of God. Catholic theology makes it its task to find out these laws, and to declare them plainly to men. Above all, it is a firm believer in their unchangeableness.

We come now to another of these great laws, the law of the spirit-will. It has been formulated by Saint Thomas, and made one of the cornerstones of his philosophy. Man here on earth, says the great Doctor, has a most changeable will. Supposing him to be in a normal condition, he is absolutely free to select his course; he chooses one thing out of many, and his choice is not necessitated with regard to any particular object. Before he makes his choice, the various objects that may allure or attract him are such that none of them is capable of fixing the will's choice, through an irresistible force. Moreover the choice once made, the will's freedom remains. A man may at once go back upon his decision; he may regret his choice the moment he has formulated it to himself.

The human will then, here on earth, is changeable both before and after its free choice.

The spirit's will is mutable with regard to any object before it makes the selection; it may do the thing, or not do it; it may choose one kind of finite advantage in preference to another. But after having made its choice, the spirit cannot retract, cannot change, cannot regret. His selection has become a fixed, unchanging state of will.

Such, in a few words, is the great law of the spirit-will. Saint Thomas, who states it hundreds of times in his works, never seems to entertain the slightest doubt as to its validity.

The law is simply one of the characteristics of a purely spiritual substance. It must therefore hold good for the disembodied human soul, as well as for the higher spirits, commonly called angels.

Like all the great laws of God, this fixity of spirit-will is a two-edged sword; it works for weal and for woe with equal efficacy. Like all other laws, it is intended for happiness; its purpose is the purpose of all work and all effort—permanence. Through it, the spirit that chooses sanctity will be a saint, eternally and unchangeably, without possibility of regret or retraction. It points to a marvelous power of decision; it is what we ought to expect from beings of such high perfection. The thought that such a power may be used for woe, that it may become eternal fixedness in an evil course, is indeed an overwhelming thought. But it is vastly less difficult to grasp than the thought that for the mighty spirit the selection of what is divine should be merely a transitory habit of will, to give way at any moment to a diametrically opposite habit. Eternal stability in sanctity is what we expect of a spirit; eternal fixity in evil is a possibility easily reconcilable with a spirit-nature. But a continual swinging backwards and forwards between good and evil is entirely incompatible with the immensity and the vigor of a spirit-will.

We ought to remember that a law of this kind is absolutely indispensable to our peace of mind, to our highest hopes; in fact, all men with higher aspirations implicitly believe in such a law, for they firmly believe in some sort of impeccability for their future state; do we not, all of us, think of the happy and holy life we look forward to as of a permanent state, from which the greatest element of instability in this life is excluded, the instability of our will? If the will were not made proof against change and sin, how could there be a genuine hope of everlasting happiness?

Scholastic theology, far from imposing a new, farfetched and abstruse concept on men's minds, is at one with the highest instinct of mankind in formulating this marvelous law. What it has done is this: it first gave the psychological explanation of this wonderful permanence of will, already assumed by mankind; then it had the boldness, or rather the common-sense, to apply the law to good and evil alike.

If the human will, or spirit-will generally, is ever to be permanently good, permanently holy, that permanency ought to be found in the depths of the spirit-will itself.

To make the law operative for good only, and not also for evil, would imply a most incomprehensible suspension of an immanent, vital spirit-law, which would be tantamount to the destruction of the spirit.

After stating the law then, let us come to its psychological explanation, though I should like to remind the reader that the explanation came after the belief in the law, and is therefore of less importance than the belief itself.

According to Saint Thomas a spirit apprehends all that it apprehends, fully, completely, directly, without any reasoning, without any tentative process; it grasps intellectually the thing in its entirety, at the first glance. Therefore whatever it judges to be best for itself, its judgment is irreformable, because it has judged with full knowledge of the subject. But not only has it apprehended at a glance the object itself, but also all the things connected with it, its side-issues and consequences. Therefore its decision is irreversible, not through lack of knowledge, as may be the case with man, but through the very completeness of its knowledge.

This is no doubt a difficult concept for us, who, according to the Scriptures, never remain in the same state. How can we imagine an eternally irreversible decision in any mind about what is best for itself? Yet it ought to be easy for anyone to understand how, there being nothing new in the spirit-mind, simply because everything to do with the object was present to the mind in its first apprehension, the judgment cannot alter.

Now, will always follows the state of the mind. If the mind's apprehensions are unchangeable, the decisions of the will are irreformable too; and this is obviously not against the will's freedom, for in every case the will always follows what may be called the last pronouncement of reason. If the human will changes, it is because reason has found new motives for change.

This then is, in a few words, the Scholastic doctrine of permanence in good and evil. It receives additional strength and clearness from a comparison, which Saint Thomas makes frequently, between man in the present state, and the spirit.

Saint Thomas enumerates the circumstances that may make man withdraw from resolutions which, at the time they are taken, seem to be final. Man is committed to an evil course through the evil instincts and cravings of the lower appetites; or through temporary and transitory allurements. Now all these things are certain dispositions of our senses, which may change and do change. Illness, for instance, has been to many a sinner a providential remedy, and he began to hate sin in its fruits. Then again, as all our knowledge is successive and progressive, new considerations may strike our mind, or old ones may strike it from a new angle. Or again, forgetfulness or distance from their occasion has ended many a man's temptations. In all conversion, one or the other of these elements is the human cause. Often they are all at work together; divine grace, without which there is no real conversion, could not enter the soul without them, at least in the ordinary course of God's Providence.

Now, it is evident that nothing of that kind could be found in a spirit; its nature is most simple, its intellect most comprehensive. I have said we ought to find the causes of the spirit's perseverance in itself, and not bring in God's miraculous action to explain it. For it would indeed be the greatest of all divine interventions if a spirit, intrinsically unstable in its will, were made by God eternally stable. No doubt it is not beyond God's omnipotence to do this, and yet leave to the spirit its own vital freedom; but it would be one eternal, never-ending miracle.

There is, in Catholic theology, one glorious source of eternal perseverance in sanctity: the clear Vision of God in heaven. To see God clearly, as He is in Himself, necessarily makes a spirit impeccable. But this supernatural cause of impeccability need not be taken into account in our philosophy of spirits. The Vision of God is something too far beyond the order of nature to be made the ordinary cause of impeccability.

The condition of the human soul in that state of transition called Purgatory makes it imperative, even from the point of view of Catholic dogma, to think of another mode of impeccability than the one of Beatific Vision. For the human spirit, in that intermediate state, is deprived of the Vision of God; yet it is in a state where sin has become an absolute impossibility.

The soul in Purgatory is fixed eternally in sanctity, because, at the moment of separation between soul and body, in other words, at the moment when the human soul enters upon the spirit-state, it has its will fixed in God, through the charity that was in it before death. The human soul makes its great choice the moment it enters into the full spirit-state. How this choice depends necessarily and infallibly on the state of man's conscience at the moment of death will be explained in our next chapter.

CHAPTER 30

The Psychology of Consequences

Catholic philosophy, more than any other, deserves the name of a philosophy of consequences. Man is the slave of his own deeds. The stress which our psychology lays on freedom makes it clear that, when one deals with Catholic principles, one has to be ready to find human responsibility as the law of this world and of the next. Hell may be an uncouth term in the ears of our fastidious civilization; but what is hell, if not human responsibility, a free result of a free will? God has left man in the hands of his own counsel to an extent we can hardly realize.

The soul makes or mars itself through its own act. This is what we mean in theology by the expression *macula peccati*, the stain of sin. It is simply this: when sin, or at least mortal sin, is committed, the soul is stained or warped in the innermost spirit-like part of itself, and so deep is that spirit-stain that nothing short of the supernatural grace of God can wipe it out.

Man may forget the act that stained his soul; he may even regret his act; but as long as the regret is merely a human regret, based on human motives, the stain remains. If the regret were based on higher and spiritual motives, the supernatural grace of God Would necessarily accompany it, and heal the spirit's wounded powers.

It may be said without reserve therefore that man, left to himself, cannot heal himself spiritually. The innermost part of his soul is made unfit for God through the act of sin.

When we say that the human soul, at its separation from the body, chooses eternally and irrevocably either good or evil, we mean this: before death, before the separation, the soul was either in charity with God or outside God's charity, owing to mortal sin; the choice has already been made, but the simple transition from life in the body to the spirit-state makes the soul's condition an unalterably fixed one.

In the case of the sinful soul, the choice of evil in this life becomes its incapacity to choose God in the next, which incapacity comes from that warping of the free will which took place when mortal sin was committed. As reprobation is essentially the loss of God, we cannot be surprised to hear that the guilty soul chooses evil; for its evil is the very act by which it turns away from God. Saint Thomas frequently uses the metaphor of a man throwing himself willfully into a deep pit; he can only be helped out by extraneous assistance. Mortal sin is an act by which the soul falls away from God, back on itself.

There is therefore a continuation of sin carried over from the present life to the next, not in the act of sinning, but in the state of the soul. As a matter of fact, that terrible collapse of the body called death makes continuation in the act of sinning an impossibility. We cannot sin in the next life as we sin now, simply because the future life is so totally different from the present; but there is a continuation of the consequences of the sin in the most spirit-like region of the soul. The soul of the sinner is thrown on the shores of eternity, a benumbed and broken spirit, and it begins its new life in these tragic conditions.

All we know of Nature's ways warns us of this. Nature is terrible in its consequences. If the human spirit, after doing evil and not repenting, after rebelling against God and not humbling itself before Him, were restored to perfect spirit-integrity through the simple fact of its being separated from the body, it would be the only exception to the law of consequences.

All action partakes of the character of that individual nature from which the action proceeds. As the sinful soul's nature is warped; when that soul has become a spirit, all the actions, all the volitions that proceed from it share in its distortion. We all expect this law to be operative in our soul for happiness; we expect that our present efforts at sanctity shall make our soul holy for all eternity. It is illogical not to apply the same law in the case of moral defilement of the will.

Why should a moment's transgression be visited by eternal punishment? Such is the stock objection. Put in that way, the objection is misleading; it assumes that wrongdoing cannot be punished otherwise than by an outside avenger. It assumes that the voluntary warping of the free will, called sin, could not interfere with man's everlasting happiness, unless God rose in anger to stop the happy mood of the unrighteous spirit, and change it into sadness and weeping.

But it is precisely here where Catholic theology parts company with superficial thought, and where it is at one with the deepest laws of Nature. Everywhere in Nature we find the law of consequences. A thing once spoilt is spoilt forever. The destruction may have taken but a moment; but its results are everlasting. If as a child, heedless of my parents' warning, I had played with firearms, and had lost both my eyes through my disobedience, the silly act would have lifelong punishment. I should be blind for life as a result of a moment's folly. A man may gamble away his family estate in one night; he brings penury to his kindred for centuries.

It is sometimes said that the doctrine of everlasting reprobation cannot be true; because Nature herself works for happiness, the final result of Nature's processes must be good. It is certainly strange to find that our great theologians make use of that very idea in their defense of the dogma of eternal reprobation. It is perfectly true that Nature works for ultimate happiness. But in order to do that, she must punish every violation of her own laws. Nature is good and kind, the mother of happiness. But individual transgressions of Nature's laws invariably produce catastrophe.

Is there any law that does more for us all than that of universal gravitation? Yet, if I laugh at Nature's law, and throw myself from a high window, that very law is my destruction.

Now the moral, the spiritual world has its laws too. You may say there must be a difference in the application of the law of consequences in its reference to spiritual and to material things, as the results differ so much in duration; one result is temporal, the other is eternal.

There is indeed a radical difference, and it is this: temporal losses may take place through no fault of one's own, may be caused by mere incapacity; yet Nature is unsparing. Spiritual losses cannot but be the result of deliberate free choice, of clear knowledge.

There is no sin there where we find no deliberate intention to transgress the law, with the power not to transgress it. There is no sin in any man through the act of another; such sin, I mean, as entails eternal unhappiness. There is no mortal sin in the ignorant, through the very fact of ignorance; there may be no mortal sin in the man blinded by passion, through the very fact of his blindness. Mortal sin is the cool deliberate choice of an evil course. There is no injustice in the law of spiritual consequences.

We must not forget another very important difference beside the one just enunciated. Nature admits of no repentance. What folly destroys remains destroyed. In the spiritual plane, however, the soul, warped by mortal sin, is forgiven over and over again during its mortal life; the soul, dead to supernatural life, is restored to life by God's miraculous grace, while still in the body.

CHAPTER 31

The Dogma of Eternal Loss, and its Theological Grounds

It is an integral part of Catholic belief that eternal reprobation awaits the human spirit that enters through death upon the permanent spirit-state, if its will be warped through mortal sin up to the very last moment of its union with the body.

That such a fate will befall the human spirit thus circumstanced is part of God's revelation to His Church. But there is no revelation as to the intrinsic reason of such an ordinance. In other words, the fact of reprobation for the soul that departs this life in mortal sin is a Catholic dogma; but there is no explanation of this tremendous truth that may be called a Catholic explanation, an explanation having as much authority as the truth it explains.

One thing, however, is certain, and in fact it is a part of the main belief in this matter: eternal reprobation is a result of mortal sin. Mortal sin is the only and the total cause of reprobation; no new and unforeseen agency of evil steps in to make the soul's lot so desperate.

This distinction is of importance, and in order to make it clear, I submit a comparison. A soldier in battle may receive a bullet in his leg, which prevents his moving freely. Owing to his inability to walk he is afterwards found and killed by a cruel enemy. The wounded leg was not the immediate cause of his death; but in a certain manner it occasioned his death. Now, it would be most un-Catholic to consider mortal sin as a mere wound, which prevents the soul from escaping some terrible powers of evil in the next world. Mortal sin is more than a wound which would put the soul at an unfair disadvantage with the evil spirits; mortal sin is, on the contrary, the total and direct cause of the soul's spiritual and irremediable death. But how mortal sin works out that great and everlasting ruination is not so certain; although the Church is indefatigable in saying that the justice of God exacts eternal punishment for mortal sin.

At first sight it would seem that we have in the expression "justice of God" the Catholic and authoritative explanation of eternal reprobation. The expression "justice of God" is, however, far too comprehensive to be the solution of so delicate and so recondite a problem. We say, for instance, that God's goodness makes man eternally happy. The term "goodness" in this proposition, though perfectly apposite and appropriate, is far from being the ultimate and precise theological explanation of the manner in which man is made happy. We know that man is made eternally happy through the possession of certain supernatural gifts. These supernatural gifts are the real explanation of how man is to be made eternally happy. God's justice, or rather the term "justice of God," stands in the same relation to reprobation as the term "goodness of God" stands to eternal happiness. We are still at liberty to give the proximate and direct causes of reprobation. The theological expression "justice of God" has many meanings. It is in fact the counterpart of the expression "goodness of God." But it also has a significance all its own, and narrowed down to the strictest meaning it stands for those acts of God in which He intervenes as Judge, directly, and as it were personally, rewarding and punishing certain definite acts of free will in His creature. God in such case is supposed to proceed by individual pronouncements; and whatever befalls the creature, for weal or for woe, is the result not so much of universal laws as of the verdict given there and then by the just Judge. It is God sitting in judgment over His creatures.

No Christian could deny to God the role of Judge; and much

of Catholic theology, as for instance Purgatory, would not be comprehensible without such divine pronouncements as to the amount of satisfaction due for offenses. But what I ask now is this: Is a pronouncement of that kind the direct and effective cause of reprobation? In other words, though we all have to admit that reprobation comes from God's justice, taken in its most generic and broad meaning, have we also to admit that reprobation is the result of God's justice taken in the exclusive and specific meaning of a direct pronouncement, based, as it were, on well-weighted points of equity? My answer is that we need not consider such an explanation as being more than a hypothesis. It is no part of the Catholic dogma of reprobation. It has been advanced by more than one theologian, chiefly in modern times, but it is not found in the theology of Saint Thomas.

Reprobation is what it is through the fact of its being an everlasting state; misery, however profound, if not everlasting, would not be reprobation. A reprobate is one who is cast away forever. Now if anything is clear in the theology of Saint Thomas it is this principle, that eternity of loss is all due to the psychological state of the soul. In the Eighty-Seventh Question of the *Prima Secundae* of his *Summa* the great Doctor enters with unmatched subtlety into the results of man's sinful action. Though he says that the eternity of loss is brought about by sin, because grave sin is irreparably in opposition to the order of divine justice, he affirms at the same time that the soul's depraved condition is itself the cause of that irremissibility of punishment. In the Fifth Article we find this golden axiom: "Eternity of pain does not correspond to the gravity of the guilt, but to its irremissibility"—*Aeternitas enim poenae non respondet quantitati culpae, sed irremissibilitati ipsius*. We know from the whole tenor of the theology of Aquinas that the soul's guilt is irreparable because, through mortal sin, grace has been banished from the soul, and had not come back before the soul's departure from the body. The Thomistic explanation of reprobation is to be found not in the direct pronouncement and act of God, it is to be found in the condition of the human soul irreparably spoiled by sin.

In the same Question, Saint Thomas speaks of God's intervention through acts of His justice, taking justice in its narrow sense; the Sixth Article is full of interest from that point of view, it is the dogmatic explanation of Purgatory. But if anything is clear in the *Summa* of Saint Thomas, it is what I might call the *created* cause of reprobation. In the Question we have cited the Angelic Doctor denies the assertion that positive infinite suffering is due to mortal sin; and when the objection is made that after all endless suffering is as bad as infinite suffering, his answer is to the effect that its endlessness is not so much a *punishment* as a *condition* of the spirit.

I may be permitted to express in a more simple way what I have said above, so that even a child might understand it. In the doctrine of eternal loss God does not threaten us with what He is going to do to us if we despise Him, but He warns us of what is going to happen to us if we leave Him.

In the next chapter I shall endeavor to give more fully the psychological reasons of reprobation. One remark, however, I think it is opportune to make here. Catholic dogma is very clear concerning the common lot of every reprobate. Whoever dies in mortal sin is separated from God eternally, and becomes a dweller in that mysterious region called Hell. But it is evident that among sinners there is endless diversity of guilt; one reprobate has sinned vastly more than another. Both reason and faith tell us that the greater guilt must be punished more severely. It is however a striking fact that we know very little as to the nature of those additional punishments, and we know still less as to the manner in which the great sinner is made to suffer more than the less guilty soul. I venture to suggest, however, that every additional act of moral depravity has in itself the seeds of its own punishment without a direct intervention of God. There will be a further chapter on spirit-penalty, where general rules will be laid down to guide us in this matter.

It may seem strange at first sight that a less guilty man should be lost as everlastingly as one who may be a thousand times more guilty. Objections of this kind bring home to us the wisdom of Saint Thomas when he says, as in the passage quoted above, that eternity of loss has nothing to do with the gravity of the fault, but is a result of the soul's state. If, on the other hand, we insist on a direct intervention of God in settling the fate of the reprobate, His justice would of course be responsible for those differences of positive punishment based on the differences of guilt.

If popular imagination has ever run wild in the matter of eternal punishment, all its fantasies have been about the individual punishments for different classes of the lost; the basic law of reprobation applicable to all the lost has had less attraction for the imagination. The less we know, the more freely we invent, and the imagination of men in that particular matter, as much as in every other concern, bears the stamp of the age that gave it birth.

CHAPTER 32

Reprobation

It is a part of Catholic belief that the reprobate spirit, either human or angelic, has a will that is eternally and unchangeably distorted, a will that is intrinsically incapable of repentance.

It would be a most un-Catholic presentation of the land of the lost to picture it as peopled with spirits that cry for mercy, and cannot find it. Time for mercy is past, chiefly because the lost spirit does not want mercy. Utter depravity of will is the feature most conspicuous in everything we know about evil spirits, both from Scripture and tradition. Their misery, their punishment, is not greater than their actual moral perversity. Their sufferings are not greater than their sinfulness, not only past but at this moment.

There is another point which cannot be doubted. The lost spirits are no longer the objects of divine grace. Even actual graces are not given them; they are left to themselves. Now, without actual graces it is intrinsically impossible for the spirit to be restored to moral rectitude. So we may safely assert that fixity of the will in evil is part of the Catholic dogma on the state of the lost. But Saint Thomas Aquinas goes one step further. He gives us the reason why actual graces are not granted to the damned. They are not granted precisely because the lost souls are psychologically incapable of receiving the touches of divine grace; they have lost that receptiveness which makes grace a congenial help. There is no opening for grace in the will of the fallen spirit.

Saint Thomas would say that the perverse spirit receives no grace because his will is intrinsically unchangeable. A less profound theologian would say that the spirit's will is made unchangeable from not receiving grace. Saint Thomas looks for the causes of reprobation in the will of the creature; other theologians look for them in the will of God, in the sense that God, in His justice, is said to refuse graces to those who did not make use of them when they were plentiful.

In other words, Saint Thomas makes the state of the created will the principal, even the unique, cause of reprobation. If God is said to inflict an eternity of reprobation, it is in this sense: God has made spiritual natures so perfect, that a wrong use of their powers will bring about results as permanent as the right use of them. Other theologians consider the eternity of reprobation as the direct act of God, avenging sin and its offense. The Angelic Doctor knew of this view, and quotes it as a legitimate argument to establish the great dogma of the eternity of reprobation. But whenever he speaks his own mind, he adheres to the psychological explanation of this great truth, rather than to the theological one. Catholics are free to hold the view they prefer. The Church tolerates both views, provided her doctrine of the reprobate's fixity in evil be adhered to. For my part, I consider the theories of Aquinas to be the kindest explanation of the dreadful mystery. Interpretations of stern spiritual facts, based on spiritual laws, are always kinder and truer than those based on the supposed direct acts of God. Eternal reprobation is merely the law of permanence in the spirit-will logically applied.

The fixity in evil of the lost spirit, human or angelic, is technically called *obstinatio*. Our English word "obstinacy" hardly does justice to the Latin term. Human obstinacy comes from narrowness of mind, from an incapacity to change views; it is a sign of weakness, not of power. There is, however, the tenacity of purpose of the strong, unemotional, intellectual man, who is rarely brought back from a design once matured; it is the fruit of strength. Yet it is only a shadow of the great spirit-law that brings about *obstinatio*. Even the resolve of a Caesar is mere weakness when compared with a spirit-will. Differences in human willpower depend on the perfection of our higher sensitive powers, not on our spiritual condition.

There is one consideration which is not out of place here. Say a man determines upon a course of action which he knows to be wrong; sooner or later physical suffering may be his wages. With the pangs of pain, his resolutions begin to waver. The power in him that resolved to do the wrong deed is different from the part that suffers pain. Pain is something new, something unforeseen. Not so with a spirit. In a spirit, the power that resolves to act is also the power that suffers the results of the act; for all its sufferings are spiritual sufferings, will-sufferings. The suffering, whatever may be its nature, is contained in the rebellious act itself. For a spirit, sinfulness and misery are synonymous terms. Punishment could never come to it as a surprise, because it cannot be punished, except in its willpower. This may be a difficult concept; but it is a perfectly certain one, and its importance cannot be exaggerated. By choosing sin, the spirit chooses its pain.

It may be objected here that this close connection between sin and its results is clear to a pure spirit; but with the human soul it is hardly true to say that by choosing sin it chooses the consequent pain. Is it not, on the contrary, a commonplace for preachers to speak of the great surprise that awaits the callous sinner when his soul enters eternity?

The answer, however, is not so difficult as would appear at first sight. The man who commits mortal sin chooses, through his very act, all the moral results of his sin. He chooses to be in opposition to the harmony of the world; he chooses shame; he chooses a state of conscience which he would not reveal to a fellowman. Relatively speaking, while he is here on earth he chooses the evil of sin as much as does the spirit. There is the same relationship in the sinful man and in the sinful spirit, between sin and its results. Now this relationship remains forever. Through death the human soul becomes a spirit; it passes into a new state. But even in that new state, the proportion between the sinful disposition and the unhappiness of the spirit is the same as it was on earth. The reprobate human spirit will then be as unhappy as he is sinful, neither more nor less.

When I say that by choosing sin we choose the pain of sin, I do not mean that in the act of sinning there is already the full realization of the sin's bitterness; this is not the case with man, and I do not think it is the case even with the spirit. But in every case, to commit sin is to realize clearly, in proportion to the nature of the sinner, the possible results of sin, and this is all we want in order to assert that any free will that chooses sin, chooses likewise the pain of sin.

It is really all a matter of proportion. Say that shame is the penalty of sin; most likely it is the greatest penalty. Proportionately, man is as much ashamed of his sin now as he will be in the spirit-state. It will be greater shame in the spirit-state, but the greater shame comes from the higher state. He will not be surprised at himself; but being greater in his spirit-state than he was in his mortal personality, his shame will be greater. If he did not become greater, he could not have greater shame.

The difficulty is put sometimes in another way. If man knew what his spirit-sufferings would be in the next world, he would never expose himself to those sufferings by committing mortal sin. People who talk like that seem to be coolly unconscious of the fact that they postulate an absolute miracle before making the sinner deserving of eternal reprobation. How could man ever realize here on earth what his spirit-sufferings will be in the next world? A spirit alone can know something about spirit-sufferings; what man realizes, in his conscience, as keenly now, proportionately speaking, as he will do in the spirit-state, is this, that through his mortal sin he puts himself in opposition to the world's harmony. The spirit-state is indeed greater than the mortal state, but freedom and conscience are the same in both states, just as, in another order of things, the charity of this world is the charity of heaven, because "charity never falleth away."

Chapter 33

Spirit-Penalty

A spirit's permanence in evil is one thing; its penalty is another, and of this we shall now speak.

Dante's vision of Hell is probably the most powerful presentment of the fate of reprobate spirits to which imaginative genius has risen. It is the most gigantic metaphor for something no eye has seen, nor ear heard. It is the boldest and most successful attempt to express the indescribable mystery in language that will startle the dullest imagination. But underneath Dante's grand drama there is the *infiammata cortesia ed il discreto Latino di fra Tommaso*, the wonderful courtesy and the wise Latin of friar Thomas. The Angelic Doctor soars as high in his intellectual concept of the penalty of the lost spirits, as the Florentine poet does in his dramatic presentment of it. While Dante piles metaphor upon metaphor, Saint Thomas is as eager to discard all foreign, all sensational, all unspiritual elements from the woeful state of the fallen spirit. His language in this matter is certainly *discreto Latino*.

I will give a literal translation of the Third Article of Question Sixty-Four, in the First Part of the *Summa Theologica*. The question asked is this: *Utrum dolor sit in daemonibus?* Whether there be suffering in the demons?

"My answer is this," says Aquinas, "fear, suffering, joy, and other such things, as far as they denote emotions (*passiones*), cannot be said to be in the demons. For as such, they belong properly to the sensitive appetite, which is a faculty in a bodily organism. But as far as these things mean simple acts of will, they may be found in the demons. And in that sense, we are bound to say that there is suffering in the demons. For suffering, as far as it means a simple act of the will, is nothing else than the striving of the will against what is, or what is not. Now, it is clear that the demons would like many things not to be, which are, and other things to be, which are not. For as they are jealous, they would like those that are saved to be lost. Therefore, one must say that there is suffering in them; and chiefly because it is in the very nature of punishment to be repugnant to the will. Moreover, they are deprived of the happiness which they naturally desire; and in many other things their wicked will is checked."

Through its relentless logic, this presentment of the lot of the reprobate spirit is as awe-inspiring as is, in its terrible imagery,

Dante's description of the Prodigal and the Avaricious in the Seventh Canto of the *Inferno*:

> From one side and the other, with loud voice,
> Both roll'd on weights, by main force of their breasts,
> Then smote together, and each one forthwith
> Roll'd them back voluble, turning again.

Renisus voluntatis ad id quod est, vel non est—the striving of the will against what is, or what is not—such is spirit-suffering!

Here is suffering, but of a kind absolutely incomprehensible to us. It is as difficult to understand as spirit-life generally. We have no terms of comparison to make it less incomprehensible. The word "suffering" (*dolor*) must be used, because it is the last resource of the human language, to express immaterial, never ceasing will-activities that are perpetually in opposition, with no prospect of alleviation.

If once we grasp this great Thomistic concept, that, for a spirit, sufferings are merely simple acts of the immaterial will, unsuccessfully, though deliberately, in opposition to the harmony of the universe, we shall think of the Catholic doctrine of everlasting punishment with greater respect; we shall admire it for its depth and its reasonableness. Eternal punishment will no longer be a stumbling block to us; the only difficulty will be the possibility of spirit-peccability. This once taken for granted, the punishment, in the sense given by Saint Thomas, is a natural consequence.

Here I may repeat what I said in the chapter on eternal reprobation, and which ought to help to reconcile our minds to the great Christian dogma of Hell. It is of the utmost importance for us to realize that, with a spirit, the power that sins is not different from the power that suffers. It might even be said that the very act that is a sinning is also a suffering, in the spirit mode of suffering, *per simplices actus voluntatis*. How those simple acts of will, meeting with failure, are suffering, we cannot understand. That they must be suffering is known more by faith than by human philosophy. Faith represents the state of the lost exclusively as an unhappy state.

The simple act of the will, eternally defeated in its object, because the object is against universal harmony, is, for the spirit, the only "sense of pain." It cannot, in any possible way, be afflicted otherwise. And this brings me to the role of Hell-fire, in the penal life of the spirit. Every Catholic has to believe in the physical reality of material elements, which are called Hell-fire, and which enter in some way into the penal conditions of the damned.

We shall see presently how to the mind of the great Schoolmen Hell-fire is instrumental in spirit-punishment, not so much as fire, but as a material element; in other words, *materiality*, as such, is the afflicting power of fire. Other material elements, such as water, could as easily have been made by God a means of affliction to the lost spirit. There is a clear statement of Saint Thomas to that effect.

I bring this to my reader's notice in order that he may see at once that our belief is mainly this: a material thing, in opposition to a spiritual thing, has some share in making the spirit unhappy. Catholic belief does not go beyond this very simple concept. The mode in which the material element is afflictive and punitive for a purely spiritual being is still debatable among Catholic divines. All their controversies on that subject are most interesting reading. Very few, if any, look for the solution to the physical and chemical activities of fire.

It may be remarked here that, if physical and chemical activities of material fire could in any possible way afflict a spirit, Saint Thomas would have been the last man to reject that explanation of the great mystery. As far as possible, he takes things literally; he never doubts the resources of nature; he is a firm believer in the stern side of things, and his views on the guilt of sin are such as to make punishment, however severe, always appear reasonable.

If then we find the great sage rejecting the "burning" as an entirely untenable theory, at least where spirits are concerned, we may rest satisfied that to a mind like his the "burning" of a spirit by fire is nothing short of a contradiction.

The proper place for the treatment of this question would have been in the last Part of the *Summa Theologica*; but Saint Thomas died before he completed his great work. His views are stated repeatedly and with great forcibleness, however, in many of his earlier works. In the *Summa* itself there are several allusions which show that he never wavered in his conclusions.

I shall quote from the First Article of the Twenty-Sixth Question in the *De Veritate*. In that particular treatise we have one great advantage: the disembodied guilty human soul and the fallen angelic spirit are spoken of in the same strain. Saint Thomas knows of no real difference in their essential conditions. There is just one possible hypothesis which might incline one to think that, after all, the disembodied soul could suffer from real burning, even where the angelic spirit could not be thus tormented. This theory supposes that the human soul, in some way, keeps its sensitive powers, or at least, the roots of them; it could therefore feel the burning of fire. Aquinas regards this solution with contempt. "If the human soul went into the next world with its sensitive powers, there is no reason why an animal's soul should not be immortal." In all respects he makes the case of the disembodied human spirit resemble the case of the fallen angelic spirits, in this question of suffering from a material thing. He then proceeds to give his own explanations, after discarding several others which are more materialistic.

Material elements detain the reprobate spirit, and circumscribe his activities. They are the prison of the spirit, and this imprisonment, technically called *alligatio*, is a most effective mode of afflictive punishment, besides being the only possible, nay, the only natural mode for a spirit to be overcome by matter.

Saint Thomas, with wonderful shrewdness, insists that in whatever way the spirit suffers from matter, it must, to a certain extent, be based upon a quasi-natural relationship between spirit and matter: *oportet invenire aliquem modum, per quem aliqualiter naturaliter animae patientur ab igne corporeo.* For even divine interventions, called miracles, are always dependent on certain pre-existing qualities in the things that are miraculously affected. It implies contradiction that a stone, remaining a stone, should be capable of thought; but not that it should rise upwards, instead of falling to the ground. Movement according to the law of gravity is natural to the stone; but upward movement, although miraculous, does not imply contradiction in the stone itself.

Saint Thomas then supposes that there is a natural relationship between spirit and matter. A spirit is naturally near matter, is in contact with matter, takes up its abode in matter, when it works upon it as a free agent, when it impresses its own action upon it; for matter is the plaything of the mighty spirit. It is natural to the spirit to be located inside a material universe, or inside a part of the material universe, as a free agent, that is to say, as one who is there just because it chooses to be there.

But that it should be so located in a part of the material universe as to be no longer a free agent is miraculous. The detention of the spirit in material surroundings is miraculous; at the same time, the miracle, like all other miracles, is based on a natural aptitude in the spirit, the aptitude to be in any place, in the material universe. To be here, or there, for a spirit, in such a wise as not to be able to leave, is miraculous.

That such detention is afflictive leaves no room for doubt. We have seen how all spirit-suffering must be a simple act of the will, striving against "what is, or is not." Through the miraculous detention, in the Thomistic hypothesis, the wicked will is indeed most effectually baffled.

Simple and direct, the theoretical considerations of Saint Thomas are to the *Divina Commedia* what the soul is to the body; they are the real inwardness of the Inferno with its ever-narrowing circles.

> Then to the leftward turning, sped we forth
> And at a sling's throw found another shade,
> Far fiercer and more huge. I cannot say
> What master had girt him; but he held
> Behind the right arm fettered, and before,
> The other, with a chain, that fastened him
> From the neck down; and five times round his form
> Apparent met the wreathed links.
> This proud one would of his strength
> Against Almighty Jove make trial,
> Said my guide whence he is thus required.
> *Inferno*, Canto XXXI

Captivity, as part of the penalty of fallen spirits, is one of mankind's oldest traditions. Saint Thomas raises it to the dignity of a metaphysical truth. It is just another application of his wonderful definition of spirit-afflictions: *Renisus voluntatis ad id quod est, vel non est.*

There is no doubt that the detention of the reprobate spirit in purely material surroundings is miraculous; it could not take place but for a direct intervention on the part of God. The material element is an instrument in the omnipotent hand of God for the punishment of the proud rebellious spirit. It would seem therefore that at last we have come upon a direct intervention of God to cause affliction in a created being. Theology puts off such direct action on the part of God, as long as it is possible. Theology never makes God the agent of suffering, if it can possibly help doing so. We must always give to suffering an explanation that makes it of created, not uncreated, origin. Spirit-sufferings, consisting of simple will-acts that are constantly being baffled in their objects, are evidently of creaturely origin; the disorder of the will is a state freely chosen by the spirit. But it would seem that the miraculous detention of the same spirit in material surroundings is an exception; and the very fact of its being miraculous would make God the direct author of the suffering. He gives the material element a power which is not natural, but supernatural, with the direct purpose of making the spirit an eternal prisoner.

Now I do not think that we are faced here with an exception to the universal law that says it is the creature that avenges the creature's sin, and punishes it. To my mind, in this case, as in every other, the harmony of the universe necessitates this miraculous imprisonment of the spirits.

We must remember that a fallen spirit is fallen only in his will-purpose: his fall means no weakening of any of his powers; it is merely the direction of his powers that is base, the aims he follows that are low and selfish. But in himself he is not altered: his intellect is as clear as ever; his energies are those which he received when he came from the hand of God, a marvel of power and wisdom; his freedom of will is as complete as before the Fall. Being the enemy of God, and jealous of God, the fallen spirit directs his powers against God, against the works of God, against the divine harmony of created things, against the law that makes all things converge towards God.

We see, as a fact of daily observation, how the laws of the material elements are never interfered with by God; how, on the contrary, they do the work of God infallibly, efficaciously. Now, we should do well to remember that the free will of created spirits is a much more potent factor in the universe from the simple fact of its being a much more excellent thing. The free will of created spirits does an infinitely larger share of God's work than the blind laws of matter. God has made the universe in such a fashion that it is self-contained, it is made up of free will and necessary laws; in all its immensity and duration, both these elements enter into its structure. The free will of one of the angelic spirits is a greater element in the world's fullness than the law of universal gravitation. Now necessary laws are invariably good; free will, on the contrary, may be wrong in its purpose; and when it is the free will of a mighty spirit that has gone wrong, it is as if the law of universal gravitation had been turned into a power of disintegration.

For such an evil there seems to be no remedy in the universe, as it is not a particular evil, but a universal one, as an angelic spirit is an essential portion of the universe. In other words, it does not seem that there is, in the created universe, any power to check completely and forever that terrible evil thing, a spirit-will turned rebellious. As Lord of the universe God has to step in. He circumscribes the evil purpose of the mighty spirit to a certain sphere, to a certain material element, called hell-fire. It is a providential disposition of God's determination to save the harmony of the world from the powers of destruction; in its results it is intensely afflictive to captive spirit.

The created spirit could never be deprived of free will itself, I mean that intrinsic vital power of will that chooses with freedom; such a deprivation would be tantamount to the spirit's annihilation; we might as well think of the spirit being deprived of intellect.

The only way to baffle a rebellious spirit is to circumscribe its sphere of action; this is, as I have said, the only meaning of hell-fire in the theology of Saint Thomas, at least in the case of pure spirits. But my contention here is this, that in circumscribing the spirit's action God is directly intent on safeguarding universal harmony. The affliction that comes from it, comes more from the spirit's deranged free will than from the anger of God. God's punitive justice does not differ essentially from His providence in maintaining the harmony of the universe; it is the creature's perverted dispositions that make the acts of Eternal Goodness so intensely afflictive. I do not remember having seen this point of view emphasized by any of the great masters. Yet it is quite in keeping with their principles.

The detention of the guilty human soul in the material element could of course be viewed from the same standpoint; for the disembodied soul has spirit-privileges both for weal and woe. The depraved human will rebels against God even in the next world, but it is eternally restrained by the fire of hell.

Clearly, what has been said in this chapter does not entirely meet the case of the human individual who is condemned to suffer eternally in his body after the general resurrection of the dead; its discussion must be postponed to the chapter on Resurrection for Woe (Chapter 45). In the meantime we must proceed to examine the Catholic doctrine of Purgatory, that transitory phase in which those souls suffer who have departed this life in grace, but are not yet ready to enter heaven.

Chapter 34

Purgatory

Writers on things spiritual have described the state of the reprobate as a great hunger and thirst for God that will never be satisfied. It would seem as if the reprobate were making the lower world re-echo their cry: "Where is God?" and that no answer should come. In this way some have imagined the pain of the loss of God. But it is evident that, if there are unsatisfied cravings in the outcast souls, these can have nothing of a high and pure nature. Hunger and thirst for God, or a desire to possess

God as the great food of our heart, is one of the highest operations of the Holy Spirit in the soul. It cannot exist without the Holy Spirit; its presence would argue great soul-perfection.

Such a description of hunger and thirst for God might be well adapted to Purgatory; but to the land of the outcast, never. A loathing for God, a horror of God, would be much more appropriate to the state of reprobation, than a desire for God. We must never forget that the state of reprobation is sin perpetuated forever.

This craving therefore must be for something else. A desire for the beauty of one Personal God is a high perfection. A desire for one's own particular satisfaction is in itself an indifferent thing; it is good or evil according as the object be good or evil. Every reprobate has his own particular object to which his will clings tenaciously. But, being an object outside the order of the universe, it can never give happiness. So we may say the cry of the lost is more like this: "Where is happiness?" and his warped conscience answers: "There is no happiness." The soul in Purgatory may be made to say: "Where is my God?" and the Spirit of God whispers: "Behold He is near, He is coming." The thirst after God comes from grace, and the quenching of that thirst is eternal life. The craving for happiness comes from the depths of human nature. The despair of ever finding it comes, in the reprobate soul, from the crushing burden of its past sins.

Our doctrine of Purgatory is based chiefly on that part of Catholic dogma which considers mortal sin to be an offense against divine justice. It is theological, not psychological, arguments we need in order to establish the doctrine. The just soul is detained in a state of comparative suffering on account of the rights of God over the human personality, and not owing to any psychological defects of which the spirit ought to get rid before he is admitted to the Vision of God.

When we see a human life coming to its end under circumstances that make us hopeful for the eternal salvation of the soul, we have often to confess to the fact that the person thus passing into eternity has been full of moral imperfections during life. We instinctively think of a state of transition for the departed soul, where all these defects will be rectified, and where the missing moral qualities will be acquired. Yet such an assumption is theologically inaccurate. We suppose the person to be endowed with sanctifying grace and divine charity. Through them the will is necessarily fixed on God; the departed soul is therefore in a state of absolute rectitude. The defects, so noticeable during life, are in that part of the human being which remains in the grasp of death; consequently the disembodied spirit is upright and pure, there is no defect or wrinkle or anything of the kind on it, nothing in fact that requires healing, its charity is perfect. This is why I said that the doctrine of Purgatory could not be based on psychological considerations. Such is the moral rectitude of the soul that enters Purgatory that it is absolutely incapable of any deflection; sin, either mortal or venial, has become an impossibility, through the perfect psychological state of the soul.

Why then should God shut the gates of heaven against the soul for a time, when there is no blemish in the spirit?

Mortal sin has a threefold effect. First it produces, in most cases, evil habits in the human organism, which make commission of further sins very easy. In the second place, it is an entire upheaval of the spirit of man, a radical reversal of natural conditions in the will, which is the most unchanging part of the spirit. Sanctifying grace departs from the soul, as it cannot dwell in a ruined spirit. In the third place, mortal sin is an offense against divine justice, a direct insult to God's Majesty, as we said in the chapter on mortal sin.

Now, the first-mentioned effect of mortal sin, as we have just said, remains with the body. The second effect is entirely healed through the return of sanctifying grace to the soul, by means of the sacramental absolution or of perfect contrition; sanctifying grace makes the soul a living soul, full of divine harmonies.

But to come to the third effect. The violation of divine justice through mortal sin can be repaired only by a person worthy of God. The reprobate in hell cannot offer to God any reparation for their sin, for the insult they have done to God's Majesty, as their state is essentially and necessarily a state of utter moral worthlessness. We may therefore easily conceive how the stain of mortal sin is radically deleted from the soul through the gratuitous infusion of sanctifying grace, and yet how God demands from the creature thus restored to supernatural life full satisfaction for the wrong done. This would by no means be contrary to that friendship which exists between God and the sanctified soul. In fact, if God is ever to get adequate satisfaction for the wrong done to His justice, it is only from His beloved ones, from those that are worthy of Him, that He can get it.

Therefore the duty of satisfaction, far from being incompatible with the state of grace, is the proper duty of those who are in grace. When we say that our sins have been washed away in the sacrament of penance, we mean it almost literally; that is to say, the stain of the soul has been wiped out. What we call the second result of sin has been annulled. But the satisfaction due to God's offended justice has become our new duty, precisely because we are now in a fit state to offer it up to Him. This is why we must do penance for the sin already forgiven. The extent of the satisfaction we owe to the offended justice of God for our grievous sins is a mystery; it takes its measure from God's wonderful sanctity and purity. Much of it, and it might be said under ordinary circumstances all of it, could be paid off through the practice of ordinary Catholic life during the present existence; but whatever is still owing at the moment of death becomes the burden of Purgatory, for He will exact the last farthing.

I do not take into account here the various mitigations and compromises in this dreadful account by means of which a small sum will pay a great debt, owing to the satisfactory value of Our Lord's Redemption. When we say that man in the state of grace is bound to repair the offense done to God by mortal sin we do not forget the atonement of Christ on the Cross; we do not overlook the fact that only the death of Christ could repair the offense of sin adequately. Christ's atonement does not exclude human atonement, as Christ's sanctity does not exclude human sanctity. Christ did what man cannot do, that is to say, give an adequate compensation for the offense.

I said that the doctrine of Purgatory is based chiefly on the Catholic dogma that mortal sin is an offense against God's justice; this of course does not exclude venial sin from being visited by purgatorial suffering, if venial sin is not fully forgiven before death. Venial sin is a disobedience. As Purgatory is only temporary suffering, it may be a fit punishment for transgressions which do not take away from the soul its capability of possessing God one day.

Perhaps more than the theological reasons for the existence of Purgatory, the conditions of the soul detained there are of interest to us. There must of course be an enormous amount of metaphor on a subject so much written about by saint and poet, especially as the *dramatis personae* are disembodied spirits. The Catholic world instinctively feels sympathy for the suffering souls and has called them the "poor souls"; the attribute has a touch of endearment. In order to be popular, a belief must of necessity express itself in figures of speech. Theology, with its rarefied spirituality, never finds popular language erroneous. It speaks truly, as far as human speech born chiefly of imagination can go. Yet it is good for the educated to be able to express the great mystery to themselves in the language "of those who know," *quelli che sanno*.

The primary fact in the condition of the souls in Purgatory is this: they are pure spirits, and as remote from sensitive impressions as the angels themselves. What is sometimes said, that the soul retains its senses radically, has to be understood in this way: when the body shall be given back to the soul in the Resurrection, the soul will have the power of causing and governing sense-life, in the re-assumed body. But it would be preposterous to think of the disembodied soul as retaining even a vestige of sense-impressions; nor would it be less preposterous to maintain that God, by an act of His omnipotence, makes the soul have sense-impressions in order to make it suffer, for it is quite contrary to the nature of a pure spirit to have sensations.

The sufferings therefore of the soul in Purgatory are exclusively spiritual phenomenon. This of course does not exclude the fact that physical agencies, like fire, may be at work on the disembodied soul. Scholastic theories on the power of fire as an instrument in God's hand to afflict a spirit have been discussed in the last chapter. We adopt the view of Saint Thomas Aquinas who considers that fire is essentially an agent of detention for these spirits. The physical and chemical effect of fire expressed by the word "burning" is, of course, excluded by all theologians. To deny its physical nature would be rashness; to make it produce the chemical effects of burning on a spirit would be an absurdity; in some way unknown to the human mind it is an agent of detention to those holy spirits who suffer most keenly through being kept, through a low element, from the God with whom everything in them is in perfect conformity.

There is a not uncommon impression among non-Catholics that we Catholics make of Purgatory an intermediate state through which every human soul has to pass, as it were, by a psychological law. Nothing could be less in keeping with Catholic theology than any such law. The fact of a soul going to Purgatory, the length of its exile there, the specific kind of suffering it has to undergo, are all free pronouncements of the supreme Judge.

Theologians are very reluctant to make of God the direct author of pain and suffering; most of the afflictions that come to the creature come to it through the creature's own act, because it has put itself in opposition to some of God's laws; but for Purgatory, theologians take up a different attitude. Its sufferings are directly intended by God; most of them are of a nature almost miraculous, requiring divine intervention. The reason for this difference of attitude is obvious. God is dealing with spirits perfect in sanctity, established in grace forever, His guests of tomorrow. The debt to be paid is of an entirely moral order, of which God alone can be the judge, as so much of the offense depended on the individual character, the knowledge and spiritual standing of every particular soul. With every one of them individually God enters into judgment. He may forgive, He may shorten, He may commute, according to His personal relation with each soul.

It is of course to be taken for granted that this judgment is carried out directly and personally by the Son of God as Man, as to Him the Father has given all judgment. It is the most noble, the most delicate part of His office as Judge to mete out to the elect of God the measure of pain that will gain them admittance to the blessed vision of the Father. This is why the saints constantly beseech Him to be a merciful Judge to them, when they come to His tribunal. "It is sweet to think," says Saint Teresa, "that we shall have Him who is our greatest friend for our Judge."

There is not one point of resemblance between the pains of the lost and the pains of the souls in Purgatory. The two states have absolutely nothing in common. The pains of the lost are the results of inflexible, universal laws; the sufferings of the soul in Purgatory are the act of God who is zealous for the beauty of His Bride. It is of great importance in our thoughts on Purgatory to give prominence to that freedom of decision which God follows as His only law in this matter. He may remit long periods of purgatorial suffering for the sake of a humble soul that implores His mercy here on earth for the prisoners of divine justice. There is nothing contrary to theology in what we read of certain saints, that through their intercession hosts of souls were released immediately. The doctrine of Purgatory leaves us wonderfully free in our speculation with regard to the duration and the nature of the purgatorial process; we need not think that fire is an agent of repression for every one of those spirits. The doctrine of Purgatory has all the attraction and all the elasticity of modern theories of the intermediate state, without their dangers; the only reservation the Church makes on our theorizing is this: no spirit has the benefit of the intermediate state unless he departed this world in charity with God.

For the sake of completeness, I must mention one more point before ending this chapter. I have considered Purgatory here as having no psychological consequence in the sense of its being a transformation of the soul. I suppose the soul to be perfect in sanctity, detained from the vision of God by the act of God, simply to make amends to God for past neglect of the divine rights. Yet Saint Thomas says explicitly that Purgatory is destined also to purify the soul from the stain of venial sin, from that psychological imperfection which venial sin necessarily leaves in the powers of the soul. This then would seem to point to a real psychological transformation to be effected by Purgatory. But the difficulty is merely apparent. The soul is in a state of unalloyed charity the moment it is in a spirit-state. Now the act by which it places itself in that state of unalloyed charity is an act done outside the body. So broad are the views of our theologians concerning Purgatory that they would call this act a purgatorial act; and therefore in this sense it might be said that Purgatory has a psychological consequence.

Chapter 35

Indulgences

The Catholic doctrine on Indulgences ought to be of easy comprehension after what has been said. If Purgatory were a process of psychological purification, it would be difficult indeed to understand how a past meritorious act of someone else could in any way hasten that purification; one might as well speak of the courage of a hero of the past being planted in the heart of a coward who is now living.

Psychological properties are not communicable. But as the doctrine of Purgatory is based exclusively on the rights of God, how is there any impropriety in the theory that God accepts an apology, we should call it "satisfaction" in theology, not only from the offender himself, but from some other person, who is at the same time the friend of God? As it is exclusively a question of offended justice, it matters little how the apology be given, provided it be given to its full extent, and provided also it be given under the conditions which God in His free will may have laid down. Another proviso would naturally be this, that vicarious satisfaction should not exclude the personal effort of reparation; personal effort is a necessary part of sanctity. One could not understand sanctity which would not be a thirsting after justice, an eagerness to give back to God what has been taken away from Him through one's personal act.

The Catholic doctrine of Indulgences provides for all these conditions. When I gain an indulgence, I gain it with the conviction that I have offended God's justice, and that I owe Him a debt, which might well be of ten thousand talents. My sincere belief in God's sanctity makes me fearful of a heavy deficit.

To gain an Indulgence is like drawing on the super-abundant satisfactions of Christ, the Mother of God, and all the Saints; in them we find perfect innocence combined with lifelong atonements in their own body. How to make their satisfactions our own belongs to the administrative powers of the Church, whom Christ has made the trustee of the spiritual wealth of the world. Thus we invariably find that the distribution of Indulgences is made directly by the living authority of the Church of God, the See of Peter; and is affixed to some spiritual work which is an effort at personal sanctity.

At this point we are tempted to embark on a little controversy with Protestant detractors. Protestantism has chosen to feel greatly scandalized at this kind of substitution; it considers it to be a fertile source of spiritual sloth. But there would be a victorious *tu quoque* to begin with, even if the charge were true. Is not the justification-theory of Protestantism based entirely on the substitution of Christ's Atonement for our own good works, and this on a scale far more disastrous to human responsibility than the substitution implied in the doctrine of Indulgences ever could be? Indulgences touch obligations which Protestantism does not even admit; for it does not believe in the duty of satisfaction after sin has been forgiven. How unreasonable of a Protestant to feel scandalized at my calling in my friend to assist me in offering due apology to the God whom I have offended; to accuse me of trying to escape my duty, when he has settled himself long ago in the comfortable belief that no such apology need be offered, even after the most grievous transgressions!

But as a matter of fact, Indulgences, far from encouraging spiritual idleness, are a fruitful source of spiritual energy. It is in the very essence of an Indulgence to presuppose purity of soul. The stains of guilt in the soul have to be washed away before there is any question of remission of punishment. Indulgences are not substitutes for personal effort, but their complement; they are a help that comes only when we help ourselves. They suppose some attempt at penance and purity of life; they suppose a complete and faithful accomplishment of every kind of virtue. Indulgences, in a word, have relation to that part of man's duty towards God that is based on God's supreme rights; a class of duties, which, as I have said, Protestantism has always repudiated.

CHAPTER 36

The Middle-State

Purgatory is not as unpopular in England as it used to be, in the forthright days of unalloyed Protestantism. A hundred years ago, it was still one of the "popish superstitions." Now it is treated with more favor. It is part of the religious belief of many who otherwise fight shy of popery. Yet it is not altogether a triumph. It would not do for us to publish it abroad, without any further qualification, that belief in Purgatory is coming back to England. Quite often, where one thought one had come across the Catholic dogma of Purgatory, one found instead the most un-Catholic theory of a middle-state, the theory of a second, third, or fourth existence, after the present life, in which to save one's soul after failure.

Both theoretically and practically, the Old Faith admits of only one time of salvation, the present life. Life, death, and judgment; one life, one soul, one eternity: these have been at all periods of Catholicism the watchwords for spiritual endeavor. At death the soul's fate is sealed forever. There is no second existence in which to retrieve one's spiritual fortune. Protestantism, whether Lutheran or Calvinistic, if anything made this stern doctrine sterner still, when it denied even the possibility of Purgatory. Purgatory, while perfectly compatible with the old Catholic doctrine about the finality of the soul's one and only existence, is at the same time that element of mercy which softens the rigors of its teaching.

The theory then of the middle-state is not compatible with the strict principles of Protestantism, though it finds its votaries chiefly among Protestants nowadays. If anything, it would be a step towards Catholicism; or rather, orthodox Protestant theology is based on principles that are the very contradiction of the possibility of a middle-state, while, strictly speaking, there is no such flagrant contradiction between Catholic principles and the possibility of a middle-state.

The Protestant doctrine of salvation is entirely based on free grace, on the choice of God, on the act of God. If God does not make His choice now, why should He make it later on, when the soul has entered upon some future existence? It looks as if Infinite Wisdom could not make up Its mind, could not fix upon the object of Its preferences. The Catholic doctrine of salvation is based on man's work, on man's internal change, on man's personal progress in sanctity. One could easily understand a Catholic preaching the doctrine of the middle-state; a Protestant would look slightly ridiculous in doing so.

The salvation-principles of Protestantism are diametrically opposed to the possibility of a middle-state; Catholic salvation-principles, as such, are not against it. Yet, Catholicism never tolerated the theory; but the grounds for the exclusion are to be sought in the Catholic view of spiritual beings, in the Catholic comprehension of man's nature, not in the Catholic view of the saving grace. As long as man can be saved, God will assist him in the work of salvation. After death, his spirit-nature does not allow of salvation, because it does not allow of change. There is this great difference between the Catholic doctrine of Purgatory and the theory of the middle-state, that Purgatory implies the momentous fact of the human soul departing this life in charity with God, while the middle-state theory requires no such soul-perfection; in fact, the middle-state theory has been invented for the benefit of those who enter the spirit-world in a state of moral hideousness; the middle-state is assumed precisely with a view to giving the ungodly soul another chance to become upright.

It is evident that belief in a middle-state comes from an anti-Protestant frame of mind; it comes from the consciousness that man must in some way work out his salvation; and in this, the theory is a move in the Catholic direction. But what is un-Catholic in it is this, that it supposes our present life to lack that importance which could make it decisive for eternity. It seems to dream of future states in which everything is greater, more advantageous, more important, better calculated to make certain the soul's salvation.

I am afraid that people who talk so glibly of a second, third, and for that matter of a hundredth existence, have never thought of the tremendously changed conditions that prevail after death. Yet it ought to be enough to remember how much of our personality remains in the grip of death to make one realize that it is impossible to talk of a second existence as something that is an unqualified improvement on the first. Death is necessarily the total extinction of all our sensitive life; sensitive life goes, with both its good and its evil tendencies; it goes as a power for sin, but it goes also as power for good.

The soul in the state of separation can only have intellect and will, two powers of extreme immateriality and simplicity. A second existence for man, then, must of necessity be an existence totally different from all our human experiences. It could never mean this, that we should then do the things we have neglected to do during the first existence. We could not do, or undo, anything of the first, the mortal existence. The simplicity and immateriality of power, which are the condition of the disembodied soul, render useless any speculations about a third or fourth existence; a spirit remains a spirit forever. If the soul's entrance into the spirit-state the moment after death does not establish it permanently in goodness and uprightness, why should it be established thus later on?

We may speak of unfavorable circumstances for the practice of sanctity here on earth. Heredity, passions, the allurements of this world, may seem so unpropitious as to entitle a man to fairer play in another world. But the flesh and the world fall away at death. There remains only the most spiritual powers of man's spirit, that part of him which cannot be the victim of adverse circumstances, as its life does not depend any more on external things.

A middle-state ought therefore to be entirely confined to that brief moment that immediately follows death. This would mean that the fact of separation of soul and body places the soul in a position of making its final choice for good or evil; or rather, it can mean this only, that one who chose evil during life should be given a chance of choosing good, the moment his soul is outside his body. But this could hardly be called living one's life over again. So great indeed is the destruction wrought by death that, were it not for the highest metaphysics and our Christian Faith, it is to all appearances an annihilation of the human personality. The spirit which, according to metaphysics and Faith, survives, is a hidden principle, an impalpable spark, in our present existence. Its survival is anything but a continuation of our present mode of existence.

We must therefore cease to think of the middle-state as an attempt at a better life. The next life is simply a state of which we have not the least experimental knowledge. The only thing we might hope for would be this, that, in some unaccountable way, the disembodied soul chooses God, turns towards God at the moment it enters the spirit-state, though the man to whom that soul belonged was a sinner to the last. This, of course, would mean infallible salvation for everybody; for why should the disembodied spirit hesitate to turn towards God, now that all the allurements of human sin are gone? The very fact of death would make man into a pure, holy spirit, however sin-stained his mortal career may have been.

Who among us could hold such a theory which in reality does away with the distinction of good and evil? Every human being, however wicked, would be made holy through the mere fact of death! Man having no other human life, through the very fact of death, cannot be said to have another chance; another chance means another human life. If to have another chance means to receive such an existence from God as was not granted during the present life, we make God responsible for the first failure, not man. If God wants man to be saved, why should He withhold those graces that are indispensable to salvation till a future state, which, in truth, is not a human condition at all?

Another unwarranted assumption of the votaries of the middle-state is that, in a future life, man will be better balanced, that his knowledge will be greater, and therefore his temptations to sin much less. But this view ignores the most essential point in the theology on the possibility and the gravity of sin. Sin is possible only where there is free will; its gravity is always proportionate to the knowledge of the sinner. God has ordered the whole universe of rational beings towards its ultimate perfection in the supernatural state; yet sin may be found in every condition, however spiritual, except there be some extra supernatural gift such as the Beatific Vision. There is always a proportion between knowledge and free will; greater knowledge means greater free will; sin is possible where there is the highest knowledge, and if it occurs then it is the greatest sin. Less knowledge means less free will; sin is possible as long as there is enough free will; but it is less, as free will is less. Evil tendencies that come from heredity and surroundings, by curtailing freedom, curtail responsibility and the gravity of transgressions.

If there is one more chance, there is no reason why there should not be a thousand more chances, in fact, endless chances, till every soul be saved. The great work of salvation would truly become a game of chance, resembling those games with which we all at one time or another have amused ourselves, which consist in getting a number of small balls within a certain compass. When you have worked half of the balls into the one groove, you try to work in the other half, by dexterously tilting the little board on which the balls run. But your efforts only result in setting free again those balls which you had already secured.

CHAPTER 37

The Sufferings of Purgatory

The sufferings of Purgatory are in a very real sense more difficult to understand than the sufferings of the eternally lost. The state of reprobation is one of confirmed sinfulness, of unceasing opposition to, and rebellion against, the harmony of the world: it is therefore comparatively easy to see how suffering may be found in the spirit of the damned, whether of fallen angel or lost soul. As I said elsewhere, it is not eternal suffering, it is eternal sinfulness that is the mystery for the human mind.

With those holy spirits, that Catholic language simply calls the souls in Purgatory, the case is quite different. Not one of the reasons that may be brought forward to establish the doctrine of the sufferings of the lost holds good for the spirits of the just. There is not, and there cannot be, in the spirits of the just any opposition to the will of God, to the harmony of the universe; they are perfect in charity.

I said, speaking metaphorically, that, for the lost spirit, unsuccessful opposition to the established order of things is the "sense of pain"; no such sense of pain is admissible in the souls of the righteous. They are under no such providential arrangement as baffles or restricts the wicked designs of a free, but perverted, spirit.

We see therefore at a glance that the Catholic doctrine of Purgatory takes us into quite a new sphere of thought. More than ever, metaphors become indispensable to express a state so far above earthly experience. The Church leaves free scope to the imagination of her children; and why should she discourage their efforts at making palpable what is so absolutely immaterial and intangible? There is no more reason to condemn the cheap print, seen in an Irishman's cabin, showing souls immersed in flames, with hands stretched out to a consoling angel, than to disapprove of any one of the Cantos of Dante. The right to express immaterial things in the metaphor of his own choice is man's oldest and most inalienable right.

Strange to say, Saint Thomas Aquinas has said very little on the nature of the sufferings of Purgatory. The part of the *Summa Theologica* which was to contain that subject was never written by him; he died before the completion of his great work. The principles that explain spirit-suffering in the lost, and which are contained in the First Part of the *Summa*, are clearly not applicable to this branch of theology. One of his principles, however, enunciated elsewhere, stands us in good stead here. It is impossible for a disembodied soul to suffer otherwise than through its being what he calls *in statu violento*, "in an unnatural state." How the souls of the just may be in an unnatural state and may yet be in a state of perfect sanctity and conformity with the will of God is again explained through a principle found in the theology of Saint Thomas. The soul of the just man here on earth has sanctifying grace; through the possession of that gift the soul is radically fit for the clear vision of God. But the human soul, while united to the body, has no clear and ardent desire to see God, because sanctifying grace is merely a remote fitness for the Beatific Vision. But the moment the soul is separated from the body, it has a direct and proximate fitness to see God. It ought to see God, in virtue of its grace and of its spirit-state. To be kept back from that vision is, in the language of Catholic theology, *status violentus*, a violent, an unnatural state; the soul is still deprived of what, by the very laws of its charity and its spiritualness, it ought to have, and this deprivation constitutes its suffering. No heavenly communication, however glorious and refreshing, could be to the soul thus constituted a quenching of its thirst.

Another principle, which I should call a secondary principle, frequently found in the theology of Saint Thomas, is this: the disembodied human soul in charity is directly and proximately fit for the companionship of the heavenly spirits. To be detained far away from that companionship is another *status violentus*, another unnatural state, which must mean suffering.

I do not think that it is possible for theology to go further than this. It is an open question whether a material element enters into the punitive arrangement of Purgatory. The theologians of the Latin Church distinctly lean towards the view that material elements have something to do with the purification of the souls of the just; but the view is far from being a Catholic dogma. If material elements have a share in the purification of the human soul in Purgatory, we must explain such cooperation in the light of the principles just stated. If material elements do punish the soul of the just, they punish it because, in some way or other, they keep the soul from the vision of God, or even perhaps from intercourse with the celestial spirits; for to be deprived of the vision of God and also of the free intercourse with the celestial spirits is for the human soul in Purgatory the only "sense of pain" we can think of. Everything connected with the purgatorial state of suffering ought to be viewed in that light.

In one of his earliest works Saint Thomas speaks of the sufferings of Purgatory very much in the language of the ordinary catechist. As I have already remarked, it cannot be said that he ever worked out that great problem. In the passage alluded to, he says distinctly that the least pain in Purgatory is greater than the greatest pain on earth. The meaning of this, from the very context, and from the whole genius of his philosophy, can only be as follows: sufferings of the spirit are acts of the spirit; therefore they cannot be compared with acts of the senses. In other words, the least spirit-act is greater than the greatest act of the sensitive powers. This is not exactly a comparison; it is simply an assertion of the fact that the disembodied soul is in an entirely different and vastly superior state, where all things have different proportions. It must be remembered that whatever the sufferings of the disembodied souls in Purgatory may be, there is a proportion between the suffering and the power that suffers. If spirit-sufferings are superior to bodily sufferings, the spiritual powers that bear them are likewise superior to bodily powers. It is simply an entirely different state from the bodily state. The official prayers of the Church invariably allude to a state of peace and tranquillity when speaking of the suffering souls.

The knowledge that our prayers bring relief to the souls thus detained comes entirely from revelation, from the official teaching of the Catholic Church; we could not know it otherwise; and therefore our intercessions for the spirits of the departed come under laws that are quite different from the obligations of ordinary human pity, as the sufferers are not human beings, but spirits.

The Protestant simply says that there is no Purgatory, because Christ did everything for us. To atone, in this life or in the next, is a slur on the Atonement of Christ. This chapter therefore is not for him, and I owe him an apology for not having made this observation at the beginning instead of at the end.

CHAPTER 38

Spiritualism

On account of the widespread attention which spiritualism periodically draws to itself, it becomes a necessary part of our philosophical and theological training to have such theories on spiritualistic phenomena as will enable us to meet the spiritualist on common ground. The best attitude for the Catholic thinker is always to concede to the popular beliefs of mankind as much as may be, and to show how the orthodox position of which he cannot yield anything is, after all, more in keeping with facts and experience than a passing enthusiasm.

The Credo of the spiritualist of all times has been that, under certain conditions, it is in the power of man to enter into a direct communication with disembodied human souls. Belief in such a power may be called one of mankind's oldest superstitions. Now, as Professor Schanz wisely remarks in his article on Necromancy in that most orthodox Catholic Encyclopedia the *Kirchenlexikon*, it would never do categorically to deny the possibility of the souls of the dead entering into communication with the living, when one considers how old and how universal mankind's faith is with regard to it.

Are spiritualistic phenomena compatible with our Scholastic theories on the disembodied human soul, supposing those phenomena to be preternatural in character? In other words, does the philosophy of Saint Thomas make it a logical necessity for its votaries to condemn without a hearing the claims of those who say that they have spoken with the dead; and this on metaphysical grounds? The moral aspect of the matter we leave untouched for the moment.

The venerable Scotus is often quoted as teaching clearly that the disembodied human spirit has powers of such a nature as to make its intercourse with man here on earth an *a priori* possibility, while Saint Thomas seems to hold that such an intercourse is an *a priori* impossibility. But a closer study of Thomistic thought makes it clear, I think, that it is quite in keeping with all the theories so far propounded in this book, to say that disembodied human spirits have the power to approach man still living on earth.

So far I speak only of the natural power of the disembodied human spirit, a power that flows from the spirit-nature of man's soul after death. There is, of course, this possibility to be faced, that such a power, though very real, is not meant to be exercised by disembodied spirits, or anyhow, is not meant to be used beyond certain limits which the wisdom of God has set to it. Here I speak exclusively of the existence of such a power. It is evident that such a power, if it be really a natural attribute of the human spirit after death, is primarily meant to be beneficent, and is above all things to be thought of in connection with the spirits of the just. We may describe it as the executive or locomotive power of the disembodied soul, and thus distinguish it from the cognitive and volitional powers which, so far, have claimed our attention; but it would certainly be difficult to define its limits. The reason, however, for not giving this power as much prominence as it seems to deserve lies at hand. It lies in the assumption that there are special arrangements on the part of God's providence limiting the exercise of such a power, or even prohibiting it altogether; limitations not to be thought of in connection with the immanent soul-life of will and intellect. Modern spiritualism pretends to know that disembodied human souls not only possess wonderful executive and locomotive powers, but also that they are practically unchecked in their use of them. Scholastic philosophy easily concedes the first point; but on the second point the Catholic Church makes very grave reservation on ethical grounds.

I have said already that Scotus grants such active power to the human soul in the state of separation. As Saint Thomas seems to hesitate on the subject, I will give a short critical survey of Thomistic thought on the matter. To begin with, in his *Quaestiones Disputatae de Veritate*, Aquinas certainly supposes in the disembodied human soul the existence of those very powers which Scotus concedes so readily. It is true the matter comes under discussion in connection with the reprobate soul. It is perhaps unfortunate that the doctrine of the soul's executive power in the spirit-world has had more of shade than of light, as it has been debated chiefly in its connection with necromancy and the imprisonment of wicked spirits. In the Twenty-Sixth Question, Art. 1, Saint Thomas speaks of the active powers of the souls of the dead with great clearness, but all in connection with the punitive arrangements that check the spirits of the ungodly. It is in the power of a spiritual nature to be united with matter as the matter's moving power or as a presence, and to depart from it, all in virtue of the order of nature; and the checking of natural power by the material element called hell-fire constitutes the torment of the lost soul. In his answer to the ninth objection he says: "The (disembodied) sinful soul is, all told, more noble than any material power, in virtue of its nature." We all know that to be more noble, in Thomistic language, means not only moral, but also physical superiority.

Now it is true that in the First Part of the *Summa* (Quest. CXVII, Art. 4), Saint Thomas denies to the disembodied human spirit power over matter and, consequently, over space. There would seem to be a contradiction, then, between the *Summa* and the *De Veritate*. But the contradiction is merely superficial. The theologians of Salamanca, who belong to the strict Thomistic school and are among the highest authorities in theological matters, give the solution of this apparent discrepancy, though they never meant it as a reconciliation of two texts. Writing on quite a different subject, without any allusion to the passage in the *De Veritate*, they say: "As the soul separated from the body does not possess through its own resources the intellectual impressions that belong to the spirit-state, nevertheless such impressions are due to it naturally, in virtue of the spirit-state, and, as a matter of fact, they are granted to it by God; thus in spite of the soul not having through its own resources power to move itself and other things [it is this and nothing else that Saint Thomas teaches in the passage of the *Summa* quoted], such power is due to it naturally (*connaturaliter*) through the exigencies of that spirit-state, and as a matter of fact such power is given to it as we said in the treatise on the Angels."[1] The passage needs no commentary. Saint Thomas constantly adheres to the principle that the disembodied human spirit is given pure spirit-power, pure spirit-knowledge, by a special act of God; the views he has on the soul's dependence on the body differ from those of Scotus; that dependence is much greater in Thomistic than in Scotistic philosophy. A soul outside its congenial physical organism is reduced to mere volition and intellection, and even that is of the most exclusive kind. So Saint Thomas speaks constantly of a divine intervention to give the human soul, when it leaves the body, congenial spirit-powers. Thus in practice there is no real difference between Scotistic and Thomistic teaching on the power of the disembodied human spirit to influence the physical world, and to come into contact with it.

It may be safely asserted that our theology on the disembodied soul makes its intercourse with the living possible, as far as the

---

[1] *Salmant.* Tomus VIII, p. 438.

soul's powers are concerned. But then there arises the question already mentioned. Is there not a direct divine ordinance, or a cosmic law, that renders such intercourse impossible? The soul has the power; but is there not established a great gulf between it and me? Is there not the hand of God warning it, or keeping it back by force? Theology has not pronounced categorically on the subject, though Saint Thomas seems inclined to believe in such a cosmic ordinance. But all that could be said against the human spirit entering into communication with man could be brought forward with equal cogency against the demon doing so.

If spiritualism meant a direct attempt to enter into communication with evil spirits, either human or demonic, then spiritualism would stand condemned before the eyes of all honest men; the ethical grounds for its rejection would then be only too obvious. But the modern spiritualist rejects necromancy and devil pacts as much as a Catholic; he says that the spirits he holds intercourse with are good spirits, and being good spirits, their comings and goings must be as much in order as the intercession of saints in Catholic doctrine. If the genuine spiritualist were ever to make the discovery that the spirits with whom he holds intercourse are bad spirits, he would withdraw at once. His whole attitude is based on the assumption that he is dealing with good spirits.

I am inclined to think that it is very difficult to bring forward absolutely convincing arguments to establish the immorality of spiritualism, in its more general and more refined aspects, on merely rational grounds. The guidance of the Church is indispensable to us in this matter. Now the Church condemns spiritualism in all its aspects as a highly pernicious practice. For the Catholic this ought to suffice. But I am afraid that for people who reject the Church's guidance as an enslaving of the mind, the lures of spiritualism are a very great temptation. It could not be maintained that the Church's rejection of spiritualism starts with the conviction that the "spirits" evoked are evil beings; such an assumption is not postulated by the Church's position in this matter. If the whole set of spiritualistic phenomena known to us was mere auto-suggestion, the Church's opposition would still be justified. It would seem as if the Church's concern were chiefly with the awful abnormality of the whole spiritualistic mentality, an abnormality that may lead to anything from lunacy to Satanworship.

CHAPTER 39

The Divine in the Human Soul

Pantheism, under various forms, has always had a strange power of fascination over thoughtful men. The reasons, however, of this attraction are not only various, but opposite in their tendencies. They might all be classed under two headings.

The first reason why man is fond of considering everything as God, or as part of Divinity, is his unwillingness or incapacity to admit Creation *ex nihilo*. To think of a Being, a Personality, making other beings, other personalities, to exist outside Itself, with a clearly circumscribed existence of their own, a sharply defined individuality; and doing all this through a free act of will, a freely pronounced *fiat*, is a heavy tax on some minds. Rather than bear the burden of such a thought, many prefer to think of the aggregate of the separate beings and personalities that make up the world as of one being, one personality, animated with one universal soul, wise through its own immanent wisdom, rich through the presence of one spirit that pervades it all. Creation *ex nihilo* once rejected, pantheism is not only a comforting substitute, it is a logical necessity.

The second class of pantheists are more interesting people; they err through a nobler instinct, a generous craving for God's nearness. They revolt at the idea of being distant from God, of being separated from God, of being distinct from God. They are bent on having something of the divine in themselves. The quickest way to do this is to declare themselves parts of the universal divinity.

I need not analyze for the moment certain spiritual affinities in these errors: the second class, the pantheists of love, unconsciously live on the metaphysics of the pantheists of negation. All I would emphasize now is this difference in the psychological causes of pantheism. Both classes of pantheists, however, are responsible for that belief in the "divine in man" which in modernized Christianity takes more and more the place of the "divine grace" of the older theology. Divine grace fulfills all that the pantheist of love craves for, without opening the door to the pantheism of unbelief. With this latter pantheism I am not concerned here precisely because it is of unbelief.

The definition, or rather description, of spirit given in the opining chapter of this treatise makes the created spirit the true and only likeness of God. He is the seal of God's image. Yet this resemblance does not make him divine, does not raise him above the spirit-plane into the plane of Divinity Itself. This is done by divine grace alone. To be a spirit might still be considered a common condition; to be full of grace is the privileged state.

With the highest of spirits, just as with man, there is the natural and the supernatural; there is that which is in him by virtue of his personality, and that which is in him through a supererogatory favor from God. As it is of the utmost importance, in our knowledge of the perfect life, to have a clear view, an exact and easy definition of the supernatural, I shall tarry one moment in order to give such a definition. The term is sorely misused in the

English language; any kind of devilry goes by the name of "supernatural."

In Catholic theology the supernatural is the state into which the created and finite spiritual being is raised by a direct act of God, distinct from that act whereby He created the spirit, following upon that first act and making the spirit inherently capable of seeing God face to face. The spirit could be a perfect spirit, even a happy spirit, without the supernatural. The supernatural is a result of God's excessive liberality, making those that are happy, happier still, with a new happiness in comparison with which the first happiness seems unworthy of mention.

When it is stated that the supernatural in the created spirit is the result of a second act of God's omnipotence, transforming the work of His own hands, it is not thereby asserted that this favor is given to every spirit He has created. Nor does it mean that it takes place immediately after the first act. As it is a token of God's excessive liberality, it is essentially a free gift. Faith, and faith alone, is able to inform us when, and under what circumstances, this second act takes place. It is the intrinsic characteristic of the supernatural to be a free gift, to which no creature, however perfect, has any claim. Our masters go so far as to say that it implies contradiction that God should ever create a spirit to which the supernatural would be a necessary psychological complement, as such a being would be another God. To make use of a common simile, in order to express the gratuitousness of the supernatural, with regard to all created spirits, high and low, I may say that we all, whether human souls or seraphs, are equally far from the supernatural, just as the astronomer who watches a fixed star from his cottage in a valley is not more distant from the bright object of his observation than the astronomer who might be watching the same star from the top of a hill.

The supernatural is inherently connected with the vision of

God face to face; it is either vision itself as in heaven, or the habitual fitness of the spirit to receive the vision, when all the other psychological conditions are fulfilled. As to the conditions under which the supernatural is communicated to the spirit, human or angelic, faith has most consoling information. It is a matter of Catholic doctrine that all angelic spirits have been endowed with the supernatural at the first moment of their existence. Our first parents before their fall never lived one moment of their life without the divine gift. In the Christian dispensation, Baptism is the certain and infallible means given by God to mankind entering into the possession of the supernatural. Baptism is like one of the world's great laws, infallible in its operation, universal in its application. Outside this great law we know one thing only, that every human creature is the object of some particular Providence that enables it to receive the supernatural. How, when, and where, is the mystery of God. One fact, however, we know. It is this: for an adult, there are certain acts of mind and will that are indispensable preparations for the supernatural, such as repentance for sin, and sincere resolve to serve God.

Coming now to a more explicit description of sanctifying grace, which is for us the "divine in man," I say that this divine grace is the greatest supernatural phenomenon. It may be remarked at once that in practice Catholic theology makes man much more divine than does pantheism. The pantheist, through the very logic of his system, is bound to keep the human individual within the bounds of limited intellectual life; man may be part of divinity, but he is necessarily and forever on a low level of it. In our theology the human intellect is raised above itself to the vision of God, as He is within His own infinite Self; for Beatific Vision is the end of sanctifying grace.

Sanctifying grace is the fitness, the divinely received aptitude in the human soul, to see God, as He is in Himself, and to be one day happy in this vision of Him. Sanctifying grace may be said to be the education or elevation of the created spirit, making him capable of seeing the beauty of God, when God will come to him and say: "Behold, I am here, the God of thy heart."

Human genius may have done its best in producing one of its masterpieces; if there be no corresponding artistic education, or anyhow a natural gift of artistic appreciation in the beholder, even a Raphael's "Transfiguration" will be just another number in the art gallery; the masterpiece is there for all to see, but what a different tale it tells the beholder according as he has eyes or no eyes to enjoy it! Such is precisely the office of sanctifying grace in the human soul; it gives the created spirit eyes for God's hidden glory; it gives him a heart vast enough to enter into the joy of a God who dwells on high. It is, then, this conformity of the created spirit with the Uncreated Spirit, enabling the creature to understand and enjoy its Creator, that we call sanctifying grace.

Sanctifying grace is therefore a permanent state of the spirit, a state destined to last forever. Just like the spirit itself, it is by its very nature unending. God never takes it away from the soul through a direct act of His omnipotence. How it may be lost through the act of grave sin on the part of the spirit, I have explained in the chapter on mortal sin. Sanctifying grace is the divine light in the soul, whose radiance can never fail; but the lamp in which it is burning may be broken to pieces; only for this the light itself would have been burning forever, as it is eternal light.

It is, I think, easy even for those to whom theology is not familiar, to see the difference between sanctifying grace and what we usually call actual grace. By the latter we generally mean a divine assistance in our spiritual life at any given moment, for a given need. It is a light dawning all at once upon our mind or upon our imagination. It makes us see a particular fact from a new point of view. It is a sustaining power given to our will, making it do things from which at one time it recoiled with horror. It is unction in prayer, joy in suffering and poverty; it is infinitely multitudinous in its workings, following up the particular bent of every character with astonishing subtlety, and conquering our most enduring obstinacies. Helps of that kind are not graces in quite the same sense in which sanctifying grace is a grace; for we know how the sinner may be under the influence of actual grace at the time when, through his very state of sinfulness, his soul's condition is the very contradiction of sanctifying grace. Actual graces are direct and transient operations of the Holy Spirit on our intellect, on our will, on our senses. They help us to do good; we may feel them when they come; we may long for them when they are gone; we may pray for them to return. Their importance is measured by their usefulness. Their adaptation to the particular needs of the individual character is one of their properties.

None of these features is to be found in sanctifying grace. It lies deep in the center of our spirit, unnoticed by man, as long as his soul is in the body. It never wanes, but it grows more intense; it is not adapted to the complexities of the individual character, but it is the uniform brightness that makes all the children of God bear the same family likeness. It is to be observed, however, that the actual graces just described are given by the Holy Spirit only with a view to producing and augmenting sanctifying grace in the soul.

Sanctifying grace is entirely divine in its origin. Through a direct act of His omnipotence, God causes it to come into the human soul. It is so high in its nature, and lies so deep in the human soul, that nothing short of mortal sin can touch it. Venial sin, committed ever so repeatedly, does not lower it, does not tarnish it. There may be a vast measure of sanctifying grace in a person of many moral failings, as long as those failings have not reached grievous culpability.

Sanctifying grace may exist, and does exist, in the soul before the soul awakens to reason, as in the baptized infant. When reason has been dimmed and obscured by some cerebral infirmity, it remains. Outwardly, those unhappy people appear to be unreasoning children; inwardly they are the living temples of God. Mental weaknesses are those at which a theologian is least scandalized; he knows how the grace of God may have hall-marked that soul for a world where one day there will be knowledge above measure.

Sanctifying grace admits of progress. It grows more and more abundant in the faithful soul, through the divinely assisted acts of spiritual life. Character building has been made the religious watchword of many in our own days. No expression could be more Catholic, provided we give it a meaning vast enough to be useful for eternity. Our divinely assisted acts, as we have described them above, when speaking of actual graces, are a constant building up of the moral character. Through them man becomes the *homo quadratus*, the four-square man, whom the ancient philosophers envied for the perfections of his virtue.

But there is a formation of character unknown to pagan philosophy and modernized Christianity. It is this: every virtuous act, prompted by the Holy Spirit, brings about in the depths of the human soul an increase of sanctifying grace; and thus makes the transitory virtuous act result in something higher than itself: a more complete possession of the unchanging participation of the divine nature. This is the only true building up of moral character according to Catholic tradition.

CHAPTER 40

The Light of Glory

In the works of our masters a good deal of space is given to what they call *lumen gloriae*, the light of glory. In fact, the space devoted in the columns of their folios to *lumen gloriae* equals that devoted to the Vision of God; and they are wise in this, as *lumen gloriae* is the one element that is wanted to make the Beatific Vision our *own* act, our *own* joy.

We shall speak of it here at some length, precisely because it has a great moral significance. For the teaching on *lumen gloriae* makes it clearer than anything else how, through the dignity of our present life, we are made capable of the vision of God, and how the present spiritual strength of our higher powers results in an everlasting capability of entering into communication with God.

Lumen gloriae, or the light of glory, is something quite distinct from Beatific Vision. Its name might be misleading; Beatific Vision could be called light of glory as it is called eternal light, because through it we see God, who is light, and in whom there is no darkness of any kind. But *lumen gloriae*, or the light of glory, technically, is not God seen face to face; it is the *capability* of the created mind to see God.

A little thought will convince us how, previous to that wonderful vision, the created mind must have been made capable of the vision; and the extent of the vision is measured by the degree of the mind's capability. Now the mind as such is not capable of this high act through its natural endowments. The human mind, or even the angelic mind for that matter, is not only infinitely distant from, but is also absolutely incapable of, the vision of God.

Therefore God gives to the mind a new power, a new capacity; He spiritualizes it, so to speak, more completely, to the extent of making it spiritual or immaterial enough to see God, if God offers Himself to the mind as its Idea.

The uninitiated would hardly be able to see why theologians insist so much on the necessity of that mental spiritualizing, previous to the vision of God. The greatest among them maintain that it implies sheer contradiction for a created mind to see God without thus previously having been more immaterialized. Consequently they hold that it is impossible, even for God, to give Beatific Vision without having first given the light of glory. What our masters are anxious to safeguard is the created mind's share in that wonderful experience of Beatific Vision.

It is *my* mind that will see God as He is in Himself, the very mind that is thinking now, while writing this; and it will see God because it will be capable through God's grace of seeing Him, as my bodily eyes are capable now of beholding this printed page. This wonderful act of Beatific Vision is the act of man, it is not the act of God. Moreover, the degree of Beatific Vision will depend entirely on the intensity of that great endowment. We shall see what our mental eye will allow us to see.

The doctrine of the light of glory is the noblest and highest instance of that essentially Catholic conviction, that man does, in eternity, not what God through an arbitrary disposition makes him do, but what he has made himself capable of doing through the grace of God in mortal life. For the light of glory is merely the sequel of sanctifying grace; it is the same entity, the same supernatural reality; the difference between sanctifying grace and the light of glory, if there be any, would be merely the difference between youth and mature age in the same individual.

This is what may be called the practical human side of *lumen gloriae*. Sanctifying grace is given to us, and given to us more abundantly, through the acts of Christian life done in the body of our mortality. We have thus a doctrine which is as consoling as it is significant of the value and importance of our Christian lives here below. Through the acquisition of more abundant sanctifying grace we acquire *lumen gloriae*; we acquire the capability of seeing God; we acquire that divine nobility of intellect, that heavenly stability of mind, that makes us radically fit for the vision of God.

How does sanctifying grace become light of glory? Separation of soul and body, in other words, the spirit-state, does not make sanctifying grace into *lumen gloriae*.

The souls in Purgatory, for instance, who are, as we know, in a perfect spirit-state, have sanctifying grace and yet they do not see God. Their sanctifying grace has not yet become *lumen gloriae*. Our masters have said little on this evolving of sanctifying grace into *lumen gloriae*. They are unanimous in affirming that *lumen gloriae* is sanctifying grace fully developed, and there their teachings and explanations stop.

We may be forgiven if we go one step further, which after all will be merely an obvious application of a principle they all admit. It is the mystery of the Incarnation that furnishes a parallel case.

There, Our Lord's manhood becomes divine through an act of God's creative omnipotence which unites the human nature with the Divine Person in a perpetual union. So, likewise, it would seem that in Beatific Vision an act of God's omnipotence unites the human intellect, already immaterialized through sanctifying grace, with God as Idea.

This act of God's omnipotence seems to be indispensable for the realization of what has been radically in the soul all along. An attentive reader might be tempted to say: "Beatific Vision is the union of the created intellect with God as Idea, while Incarnation means the union of human nature with the Divine Person. Beatific Vision and Hypostatic Union seem closely allied, seem to belong to the same plane of spiritual possibilities." Our masters readily grant this similarity. They consider that nothing short of this similarity could make us the brethren of the Incarnate Son of God. "For now we are called the sons of God, and are such, though it has not appeared yet what we shall be one day; but when He shall appear, we shall be like unto Him, because we shall see Him as He is" (1 John 3:1–2).

CHAPTER 41

Beatific Vision

I think I am right in saying that most men have made for themselves a hereafter in keeping with their special spiritual temperament. We all have our own Paradise. But as our minds change, and our needs take new forms, we may change our views of Paradise; we may get tired of views which we have long entertained and cherished on this matter.

Now there is the Catholic theology on heavenly happiness, wonderfully sober in its majesty, and sooner or later it is the thing we all want, in order to find satisfaction for our mind and heart. The vision of God is the central joy of heaven. It is not merely a theological opinion that the spirit of the saved will see God forever, it is a matter of Catholic Faith. Both tradition and explicit definitions of general Councils have raised it to the level of a dogma. To doubt it is secession from the Church of God.

There is almost unanimity among the masters of sacred theology in the explanation of the mode in which man is raised to the vision of God. It may be said that this doctrine, whose personal importance for everyone is simply immeasurable, is one of the best defined and best understood articles of faith.

We find too, in practice, that it is a doctrine easily grasped, even by the simple; a doctrine that appeals even to the child; and so it ought to do, as Beatific Vision is the direct result of all the acts of our higher life here on earth.

The very simplicity of this doctrine gives it great power for strengthening the moral man, for making us more spiritual; for we are spiritual, not through pious imagery, but through the assimilation of simple far-reaching principles. The vision of God, as the term implies, is the seeing of God, not with the bodily eyes, of course, but with the mind.

The main idea conveyed by the term "Beatific Vision" is this: it is God, as He is in Himself, who is seen by the mind; it is not a mere image of Him, a mere idea of Him, however clear; it is Himself. It is a direct, unintercepted gazing on God's beauty.

Our masters are aware of the fact that it is in the power of God to give the created mind very vivid knowledge of Himself; God has endless ways of making the created mind know Him; but all these ways fall infinitely short of Beatific Vision.

In Beatific Vision, according to the profound doctrine of Saint Thomas, God Himself becomes the idea which is in the mind of the elect. All our cognitions are ideas, of more or less extent and clearness, that come to our mind through a hundred channels. We see clearly that the idea of a thing is not the thing itself; for the thing is outside me, while the idea is in my mind, and makes of my mind, from an unknowing mind, a knowing mind.

Now, says our great master, in Beatific Vision there is no such idea of God, as distinct from God, to stand for God in my mind. God's very nature is the idea. In fact God has to be the idea, for nothing could ever do duty for God Himself in my mind.

If I am to know Him as He is, He must be Himself the idea that makes my mind a knowing mind. We easily see how knowledge, in the words of the Schoolmen, is invariably based on the idea of the thing being in the mind, while the thing known has its existence outside the particular mind.

I may have a constant thought of a person dear to me, a thought that is representative of many of the attractive qualities of that person; but I see all along that the person is outside me altogether.

It does not seem possible even for a pure spirit to think of a fellow-spirit otherwise than through one of these representative ideas. No spirit, in his particular personality, could be actually in the intellect of another spirit. God alone is given by theologians what they call *illapsus*, the power of being personally within a created mind. Both the existence of such a power, and the exclusive possession of it by God, are theological certainties; in Beatific Vision God makes use of that power.

The eternal hills rise higher and higher, and the thoughts of God on their summits are getting purer and purer; but they are mere thoughts of God, they are not yet God. They are mere ideas of God.

These thoughts are so high indeed that if one of them were communicated to us mortals, we should feel as if we had been lifted bodily to the Throne of God; yet even on those high summits, the created mind has not yet met with God.

In Beatific Vision, God Himself is the idea, God Himself is in the mind; and here we have the radical difference between Beatific Vision and every other kind of divine knowledge, however sublime.

A comparison might again be made between Beatific Vision and the Incarnation; the comparison is suggested more than once by Saint Thomas himself, and I hope that by making use of it I am not explaining a recondite thing by a more obscure one. I think most readers may be able to follow the comparison.

In the Incarnation it is not a created or finite resemblance of the second Person of the Trinity that is united with manhood; it is not some wonderful supernatural gift that makes this human nature to be divine; it is the Second Person of the Trinity, directly united with human nature, without an intermediary grace, that makes Christ's human nature to be divine. For created supernatural gifts could only make it holy, but not divine. The Uncreated Person of the Word alone could make it divine. So likewise in

Beatific Vision the Uncreated Godhead alone, in the created mind, makes this latter know God. No created idea, or representation of God, could do it.

From what precedes we shall readily fall in with this theological conclusion: the vision of God, enjoyed by the Blessed, is the vision of the totality of God. God's perfect simplicity of nature makes this conclusion a necessity. By this we mean that the Blessed behold intellectually not only all and every one of God's attributes, but also behold the Trinity of God; in one word, every elect beholds the infinity of God, though he does not behold that infinity with infinite intellectual keenness.

This distinction will be made clearer in the next chapter. God is infinitely simple; but we know that scripture and theology have, as it were, seen various characteristics in God, called God's attributes. Goodness, sanctity, justice, omnipotence, mercy, and so on, all infinite in intensity and extent, are some of the attributes of God. These designations are not mere forms of speech; they are founded on the fact that God's infinite simplicity is also infinite fullness and multiplicity. Thus, for instance, what we call divine justice is not at all the same thing as divine mercy; and the claims of divine justice are not the same as the claims of mercy. In Beatific Vision, then, every one of those known and unknown attributes of God is beheld by the glorified mind, though not, as already said, with infinite keenness of mind.

It would be entirely against the characteristics of the Beatific Vision to suppose that in it anything in God is only half unveiled to the mind, leaving it to the mind to try and guess the hidden part. All that is revealed is revealed most clearly, so as to give complete mental satisfaction to the intellect.

If some of the elect know more, their privilege does not rest on a clearer perception of a thing, seen more dimly by the less exalted saint. It would not be vision for the less exalted saint if he saw only dimly.

The privilege of the higher saint is this: to be admitted into entirely new mysteries which the totality of vision spoken of above does not include. How this is possible I hope to explain to my reader presently.

CHAPTER 42

Degrees of Vision

It is one of the deepest convictions of the Catholic heart that eternal life is shaped by temporal life; that every good deed done in the body has its particular reward in a new happiness given to the human spirit in heaven; that every act, inspired directly or remotely by the love of God, is an eternal acquisition that cannot be lost if the soul perseveres in the state of grace to the end.

Equality of state and happiness in heaven is a thing repugnant to the Catholic mind; and to acknowledge that star differs from star in heaven is the delight of the humble and generous heart. These inequalities, based on inequalities of merit acquired during mortal life, will be found, no doubt, in every branch of celestial glorification. A martyr, for instance, will have at least a partial superiority to the confessor who came into the heavenly country without having been asked the price of his blood. The act of fortitude included in martyrdom will be a partial superiority, though the martyr need not be superior to another elect in every respect; but he is superior in the glory that comes from heroic fortitude.

When we speak of superiority or inferiority amongst the Blessed, we speak of absolute superiority and inferiority, of differences in the Beatific Vision. It is the Beatific Vision that gives the saint his eternal position in the house of God. The reading of the lives of the saints has familiarized us with the doctrine of the varying degrees in the Beatific Vision. Who, for instance, has not heard of the protestation of Saint Teresa, declaring that for one more degree of Beatific Vision she would be ready to live and fight and suffer to the end of the world, deeming an additional degree in perfect vision a reward exceedingly great?

But here we are confronted by the difficulty already insinuated in our preceding chapter and held over till now. With all theologians we have asserted that it belongs to the very essence of the Beatific Vision to reveal the totality of the Godhead to the created mind. No elect sees God without seeing everything of God. Where, then, is the differentiation? It is perhaps one of the most vexed questions in sacred theology. The elect with greater merits sees God more perfectly, this is Catholic faith. That every elect sees Him entirely is likewise Catholic faith. But no elect comprehends Him fully; this is a third article of faith, which attributes to God, and to God alone, a full comprehension of Himself.

Saint Thomas does not desert us in these high regions, and his solution of the theological difficulty is a very persistent one, found in all his writings. It may be broadly stated in the following manner, though in stating it we follow more his spirit than his actual words. In God there are those things that could not be otherwise, precisely because He is God. They are what are called His necessary attributes, and these are seen to their full extent by all the elect. But in God there is free will; He acts, because He chooses to act; He is not compelled to act in this way or that; it is a part of God, which entirely escapes the eye of the beatified beholder as such, because, being acts of His free will, they do not follow necessary laws. Thus, it is God's free choice that the Incarnation should have taken place at such and such a time and under such and such circumstances.

We all see how these free acts of God, infinite in number and possibility, constitute inside God, as it were, something new, precisely because they are free. Now, it is the constant teaching of Aquinas that admission into this divine privacy, into the knowledge of God's free choices, past, present, and future, constitutes the higher reward or the higher vision. They are called the secrets of the counsels of God. The Blessed Mother of God reigns supreme in the Beatific Vision, because she is admitted more completely than any other creature into the hidden dealings of God with the created universe.

It is, I think, easy, even for the non-theological mind, to see how this distinction between what is necessary in God and what is free will in God, establishes a clear and certain division between simple vision and comparative comprehension. It shows how the totality of God may be seen, and how at the same time much may be hidden, as God's free acts, from the very fact that they are not so much a part of God's nature as His free choice.

Such, then, is the solution of the Angelic Doctor. All the same, it took the writer of this book a long time to find rest and satisfaction in this solution. It had always seemed to him that a merely more abundant knowledge of free acts could not adequately constitute a state of superiority for one who has toiled more abundantly during life; and all the more as God's free dealings with His created universe could be made known to a created mind, outside Beatific Vision, through the communication of ideas that are not God Himself. But more assiduous study of the great *Summa* has convinced him of the wisdom of Saint Thomas Aquinas.

Free acts in the creature are transitory things; to know them may be instructive, but it is not an illumination of the mind, it is not a raising up of the intellect to a higher plane of thought; they are, so to speak, mere history, mere facts. But such is not the case with the free acts of God. They are eternal wisdom; they are eternal justice; they are, as Aquinas says somewhere, though not in connection with this matter of the Beatific Vision, the rules of Goodness. To know one more of these acts is to know better not only what God does, but what He *is*.

This difference between the created free act and God's free act makes it quite clear why Saint Thomas made higher heavenly life consist in more copious knowledge of the determinations of God's free will.

CHAPTER 43

Participated Eternity for the Human Soul

It has always been a question with pious and thoughtful people: "How is there no such feeling as monotony in eternal life, and how, in the vision of the unchanging God, is there eternal freshness, eternal interest?" But we must rise above imagination, and try to understand something of the wonderful unchangeableness of the Beatific Vision.

"To see God forever" is a phrase that does not give the whole content of the theological doctrine. We must not think of that glorious life as of an endless succession and repetition of the same act, so that to see God forever would be merely to see Him day after day, forever and ever.

The vision of God is eternal life. Now our masters consider that the term "eternal" here has a technical and exclusive meaning. We must define eternity thus: the actual, total, and unchanging possession of life. Unchangeableness, and totality of all happiness in that unchangeableness, is God's eternity. It is not so much an endless life as an unchangeable life, unchangeable because it is a complete and absolute totality. Our eternal life then, our eternal vision of God, is eternal in the sense in which God is eternal.

Our masters call it "participated eternity." They consider that in this highest of intellectual regions, the vision of God, a creature actually shares a divine attribute, eternity of act.

Thus the act of Beatific Vision is not a successive act, not an everlasting act, in the sense in which any spiritual creature is everlasting, because indestructible. It is more than all that: it is eternal, as God is eternal; unchanging, because it is, all at once, the totality of every good.

No other act of the spiritual creature, however perfect the creature may be, has that characteristic of eternity. They are all transitory, successive acts. They succeed each other forever and ever.

The act of Beatific Vision alone is above the divisions of time, and has a stability far superior to the stability of the *aevum*.[1] Our masters do not see any psychological impossibility in a mind having one eternal act, while having, concurrently, many successive acts of a lower order, subject to the rules of ordinary mind-time.

We have in Beatific Vision mind-eternity, which alone can make a perfectly happy state. Frequent reflection on this possible eternity, for our created, ever-changing minds, may become for us the source of great spiritual strength.

We might find it hard work, at the beginning, to find satisfaction in the prospect of an unchanging act. Our whole earthly life is a succession of new experiences and emotions.

But the emptiness which constant change of emotions leaves behind will make the thoughtful happy in the belief in a state so perfect that its eternal stability is its eternal newness.

The theological doctrine of Participated Eternity has brought us to the highest summit of human perfectibility. To see God is itself wonderful; to see Him through an eternal act is an even greater wonder.

[1] The *aevum* is the mode of existence experienced by the angels in heaven. "The *aevum* differs from both time and eternity, as something existing in between the other two... In sum, time has before and after, the *aevum* does not have in itself any before and after but these can be associated with it, and eternity has neither before nor after, nor does it allow for these." *Summa Theologica*, Q. 10, Art. 5. –Ed.

CHAPTER 44

Spirit-Animation or Resurrection of the Body

In the opening chapters of this book we already made a distinction in the human soul between the soul and the spirit, not, of course, in the sense of a twofold entity, but of a twofold state. While the soul spends itself in animating the body, it might be said to act only as soul; for by soul we understand primarily an immaterial substance animating an animal organism.

In the state of separation the soul is only spirit, without an actual or even possible animating office. It is in this sense that our masters distinguish between soul and spirit. They repudiate, as we well know, any plurality in the immaterial substance of the soul.

I said just now that the soul in a state of separation is devoid not only of an actual, but also a possible, animation; we take animation here in its active sense. This apparently seems to contradict the dogma of bodily resurrection, when the soul is believed to come back to its body to animate it again. But our answer is readily at hand. As one of our great masters, Cajetan, says, in the resurrection the human soul gives life to the body, not as a soul, but as a spirit. This is a deep and important distinction, well calculated to explain the Christian dogma of the resurrection of the body as contained in the Epistles of Saint Paul.

One thing is certain: though we may consider the state of separation as less advantageous than the state of union between soul and body, yet the fact of disembodiment has given to the soul new attributes, which cannot be lost, as, for instance, inflexibility of will, and the capacity of knowing the spirit-world directly as it is in itself.

Mutability of purpose, and the soul's ignorance of its own self, came from the union with the body; through the separation it came to have a clear knowledge of its own essence, to make of its own self the medium through which it considers all other things. These are some of the exclusive features of the spirit-state, and they are, as I said, the soul's portion forever.

So when the hour for re-animation comes, an hour the Father alone knows, it is evident that the human spirit is in a condition entirely different from the conditions under which it first animated the body, at the origin of the human individual. That is why our masters say that the soul animates, not as a soul, but as a spirit, in the resurrection of the flesh.

In the first animation the law is this: the soul is made conformable to the body (superior to it, of course, as spirit is superior to matter, yet conformable to it), so as to make of the two a harmonious compound. The body comes first, transmitted as it is by the laws of heredity; the soul is created by God to animate the organism. Our masters speaking of the role of the organism to which the soul comes call it a *causa occasionalis*; that is to say, God creates the soul to complete His own laws, and created causality is for Him the occasion for that completion. But Saint Thomas is most explicit in stating that God adapts the soul to the perfection of the organism, so that the soul coming from His hand is more or less perfect according to the perfection of the organism. He does not say in what this "more or less" consists; only he teaches for our consolation that it is not a "more or less" in every respect, but only in certain respects.

Thus, he says, with the simplicity of a great genius, a man of small stature may be a better or a cleverer man than the one of large stature; yet this does not prevent the giant being superior to the dwarf in stature. I mention this difference, which in practice need not disturb us, to illustrate how our masters in their wisdom made the body the measure of the soul. In their teaching on the resurrection of the body, however, they adopt the opposite law of action, and make the disembodied spirit the measure of the body.

The soul returning to the body gives that body everything, even its individuality, or what might be called, more loosely, its personality. This is the express teaching of Cajetan. It is a great concession on the part of a Scholastic of such eminence as Cajetan to say that the soul, the spirit, should give the body its individuality, when it was the body that gave the soul its individuality at the first union, the union of the mortal days.

According to a unanimous consensus of Catholic theologians, when man is first made through the laws of generation, the body is at least the occasion for the soul to be made, and to be made this particular soul, by God. On the contrary, when man is re-made at the resurrection, his body is made this particular body through the soul that comes to it or returns to it.

I make a distinction here between coming to the body and returning to the body. For Cajetan supposes that there are cases where the matter of the previous body is not to be found anymore, and when God in His omnipotence supplies the matter for the new body. In that case Cajetan considers that the soul has enough resources in itself to give that body the individual character that makes it resemble the original body.

The possible circumstances that could bring about such an entire disappearance of the original bodily material are cleverly suggested by Cajetan. Suppose, he says, generation after generation of men have fed almost exclusively on human flesh; there must be a passing of one body into another body. In an extreme case like this, God has to supplement the missing flesh, but the soul has the power to it such characteristics that it becomes the self-same human individual that it was in the days when it walked this earth.

CHAPTER 45

Resurrection for Woe

The resurrection of the body of the elect is the highest triumph of God's grace. There is comparatively little difficulty in believing in it; it is a sequel of the whole of the supernatural economy, which is essentially based upon Our Lord's Resurrection.

But this doctrine of bodily resurrection has its dark side too; it is a two-edged sword. It is a matter not only of theological certainty, but of Catholic faith, that the reprobate also will rise in their bodies, to bear in their flesh the fruits of their deeds.

It would seem as if resurrection were one of God's primary ordinances to be universally effective for the happiness of mankind. That for some it should become greater confusion and suffering is not the fault of the divine ordinance, but is owing to the perverted state of the soul.

Not to admit resurrection for the reprobate means shipwreck to faith. The theological difficulties of the doctrine are more considerable, however, in the case of the reprobate than in the case of the just. We can easily understand how, for the elect, God endows their body with gifts and qualities that make them the fit instruments of the glorified spirit. No such direct influence of the divine action exists for the reprobate spirit. Reprobation means, as we know, utter rejection.

That the risen body of the reprobate is given immortality is evident from the very fact of resurrection. How this immortality is given to it is a more difficult problem. Saint Thomas, though he be so emphatic in declaring that it is the very nature of the risen body of the reprobate to be immortal, does not admit of a direct and continuous act of God keeping the body everlastingly in existence merely for punitive purposes. Such a direct act on the part of God is entirely against the genius of Scholastic theology. Saint Thomas finds the explanation of the incorruptibility of the human body in the entirely changed condition of the material universe. It goes without saying that the bodies of the reprobate are perfect, as far as the organism is concerned. Nature's work in the first production of the human body is often hampered; it rarely produces a perfect body. Not so in the resurrection, where the only law is God's omnipotence and the spirit's activity. It is most untheological to think of the dwellers in the region of darkness as of horrifying monstrosities. But if incorruptibility and natural completeness and perfection are the conditions of the bodies of the damned, these bodies are not above passivity, I mean the capability of suffering.

Here once more Christian dogma must overrule sentimentality. That fire is a source of suffering to those risen bodies must be held by every Catholic. But even here the explanations of Saint Thomas lift the dogma to comparative immateriality. The action of the elements on the reprobate body must differ entirely from the action of the elements on our mortal body here below. As in the case of spirits, we have to admit here the reality of the fire. But we admit more: an action of the fire that causes bodily suffering. Saint Thomas, however, is explicit in stating that it is a spiritual action, not a material action. He holds that the fire has a real effect, an effect which he compares with that of light on the eye. It is a real effect, yet it does not alter the eye, or change its state. Such, he says, is the action of hell-fire. Beyond suggesting this explanation he teaches nothing.

With this, Christianity may face the world and its sentimental humanitarianism. After all, what is Christianity but an intense belief in human personality, making of man a responsible being, to choose for himself, to shape his eternity? In the eyes of the humanitarian, God is very much like a man whose sole office is to throw food to flocks of irresponsible geese; to feed and to fatten his poultry is all that man is expected to do.

To find fault with the finalities of Catholic theology is to ignore the conditions for salvation. Moral responsibility is never greater than knowledge. Higher knowledge will mean higher responsibility.

There would always be the same proportion between knowledge and responsibility even after a thousand migrations, or incarnations, or phases of existence, if such were granted.

There is no more reason to give three chances to a creature than one, considering that every time man's salvation ultimately depends, not on knowledge or circumstances, but on free will. But, I dare say, with many there is some such view as this at the back of their mind: the individual who has made, as the saying goes, "a mess of his life," when he comes into the next world realizes what danger he has escaped, and instantly starts retrieving his fortunes and making amends. But who does not see that there is a flagrant begging of the question in this very assumption? How could man become more convinced after death that his sinful mortal career has brought him so perilously near eternal loss if, as our friends say, the ordinances of a kind Providence bestow on him as many chances as he could possibly desire? In that case there would be no danger in making bad use of his first chance.

It may safely be asserted that Catholic theology, even in this matter of the bodily resurrection of the reprobate, has no other disabilities or sufferings for them except such as come from the very conditions of the material universe in which they will find themselves. They are simply part of the world to which they clung, and above which they never rose.

There is among the minor works of Cajetan a sermon preached

on the First Sunday of Advent in the year 1504, in the presence of Julius II and his court. It is a masterpiece of theological conciseness, and one cannot help admiring men who would listen to discourses of such profundity. In that sermon Cajetan explains, to the satisfaction of the vigorous Pontiff, spirit-penalty and the action of hell-fire, in the same way in which I have tried to explain those great truths to my patient reader.

CHAPTER 46

The Human Soul and the Angels of God

From the very beginning of this book we have emphasized the doctrine of Saint Thomas that the human soul after this mortal life enters into a pure spirit-existence. I shall now give some of the theology of the Angels as far as it has any connection with the destiny of the human soul.

The theology of the Angels is far from being of merely academic interest, a kind of intellectual curiosity. It has a practical bearing, the importance of which could hardly be exaggerated. Our life, after the dissolution of the body, is to be intimately connected with the life of the Angels. The highest perfection of the redeemed and glorified soul is the vision of God. Next to that, there is the vision we shall have of the Angels of God. To see them as they are, to share their life, to be of their company, all this belongs to the glorified soul.

It might even be said that this companionship with the heavenly spirits is more within man's claims than the blessed vision of God. We fight bravely here on earth, while we are in our mortal tabernacle, against the errors, the snares and fascinations of our senses; we fight in order to be spiritual, when all that is base in us

tends to make us animal. To be admitted into the society of the
spirits that were perfect from the beginning seems to be the most
appropriate reward. To be admitted to the vision of God Himself
is due only to the possession of gifts in our soul that are in us
directly through the indwelling of the Holy Spirit. We find this
hope of an admission into the spirit-society even where the hope
of attaining God's vision does not exist; there is indeed a school
of non-Christian philosophers to whom supreme happiness is the
contemplation or vision of what they call the *formae separatae*, the
beings free from matter. They understand with the Christian
philosopher that the effort of the ascetic, who strives against the
lusts of the flesh in order to be spiritual, must be crowned with the
vision of, and unveiled intercourse with, the most perfect spirits.

Christian theology has raised these refined instincts of human
reason into an article of faith, that man's recompense will be life
unending with the Angels. There is, of course, something higher
than that which will be given to man: the vision of God. There
will be joys lower than that, as for instance those joys that come
to the glorified body. All the same, it remains true to say that the
human soul, as soul, is primarily destined to enter into the angelic
society. This is due to it for keeping itself spotless from the world.

We shall do well to recall how much Our Lord insists on this
aspect of the question: "For he that will save his life shall lose it:
and he that shall lose his life for My sake shall find it. For what
does it profit a man, if he gain the whole world and suffer the loss
of his own soul? Or what exchange shall a man give for his soul?
For the Son of Man shall come in the glory of His Father with His
Angels: and then will He render to every man according to his
works" (Matthew 16:25–27).

An Angel is greater than the material world with all its glories;
so is the soul, if it but understand its dignity. But if it degrade
itself to possess the world, the Angel scorns it; and whither shall

it go, if the scorn of the Angels is upon it? The world which it tried to grasp will not satisfy its hunger; it was made for the Angels; woe then to it, if it does not find the Angels.

"He that shall overcome, shall thus be clothed in white garments: and I will not blot out his name out of the book of life. And I will confess his name before My Father and His Angels" (Revelation 3:5).

"For he that shall be ashamed of Me and of My words, in this adulterous and sinful generation, the Son of Man also will be ashamed of him, when He shall come in the glory of His Father with the holy Angels" (Mark 8:38).

"And I say to you: Whosoever shall confess Me before men, him shall the Son of Man also confess before the Angels of God. But he that shall deny Me before men shall be denied before the Angels of God" (Luke 12:8–9).

Here then, and in the preceding passage, our Blessed Lord identifies eternal loss with exclusion from the angelic society. Not to be among the Angels is for the soul failure to arrive at its natural goal. It will be a bitter thing for the human soul to have lost God; but this great and useless regret will leave room for another despair, incomparably keen, that of having been rejected by the Angels for whose society it was primarily made.

It is a common opinion among theologians that the elect of the human race are destined to take the place of the fallen Angels. In what way this happens it would be difficult for us to define. This could hardly be understood otherwise than of gifts exclusively supernatural; in other words, the elect of the human race are destined to possess those revelations of God's countenance which were meant for the spirits that fell from His favor.

We must bear in mind, however, that there is no theological tradition that limits the number of the elect from the human race to the number of "empty thrones" left vacant through the fall of the rebel angels. Nor would it be theologically correct to say that man's admission into the angelic society comes through the fall of the proud spirits. It is in the very essence of the human soul that we must look for the origin of that exaltation.

What we have said in a previous chapter concerning the spirit's remoteness from matter will make us careful when we try to represent to our own mind the way in which we expect to take up our abode among the heavenly spirits. It is evidently something that is all of the spirit. Local abiding among them is out of the question; it is merely a metaphor.

How then shall we be made the fellow citizens of the blessed spirits? There is one way only: by sharing in their knowledge and in their ways of knowing. This is why our masters in sacred doctrine are unanimous in teaching that before we receive the vision of God, we have the angelic knowledge.

"But they that shall be accounted worthy of that world and of the resurrection from the dead shall neither be married nor take wives. Neither can they die any more; for they are equal to the Angels and are the children of God, being the children of the resurrection" (Luke 20:35–36).

Equality with the Angels must necessarily mean intellectual equality, as all the attributes of spirits are intellectual, or connected with the intellect.

Thus it will be possible for the elect to converse with the Angels in "their own tongue." The question might be asked how the human mind is made to possess this knowledge, so far superior to its own plane. Saint Thomas thinks that it is in the power of the heavenly spirits themselves to communicate it to the human spirit. God, and God alone, can give Beatific Vision; but it would be a great limitation to the angelic powers if the communication of their own knowledge were not left to them. I must note, however, that the mode in which angelic knowledge is given to the elect soul is not a matter of such absolute certainty as is the fact of such a possession. We may, if we choose, hold the alternative view that the human intellect is raised to the angelic plane by a direct act of God. The first view, however, ought to commend itself more to the philosopher's mind, as secondary causes ought to be credited with as much activity as possible; for God shows forth His power in making His creatures powerful.

Where is the tongue to sing worthily the blessedness of this aspect of our eternal destiny? "Blessed are they that hunger and thirst after justice: for they shall have their fill." Not a shadow of error, not a vestige of ignorance, not the faintest sign of injustice, through all that mighty spiritual world! And all that, after escaping from a world steeped in mendacity, error, prejudice, where gigantic lies and monstrous injustices make the life of the children of God a burden! Let it be of little account to be misunderstood by this adulterous generation! Our judges will be the holy Angels of God.

There is one more consideration which finds its natural place here: numerous as the Angels are, they are not just a huge crowd, but a hierarchy, both in knowledge and love. Consequently, they will all enter into our life, be part of it, and contribute towards the fullness of it. With mankind, we feel daily more and more how the individual is isolated from his fellowmen, how the generality of men are nothing to us, have no share in our lives. They come and go, and we remain as if they had never existed. Not so in the world where we shall be equal to the Angels. As hierarchy is part of their nature, to be with one means to be with all of them.

This is the way in which we come, through the Blood of Christ, "to Mount Zion, and to the city of the living God, the heavenly Jerusalem, and to the company of many thousands of Angels" (Hebrews 12:22).

CHAPTER 47

Guardian Angels

Belief in the constant presence of a celestial spirit with every child of man, and its unceasing guardianship over him, was bound to make the fortune of Christian art. From earliest childhood we have been familiarized with pictures in which a youth, with a beauty not of this world, walks majestically and recollectedly at the side of his human protege.

It is always a gain to our faith if we succeed in finding the true doctrinal and theological meaning of the symbols that were the food of our childish minds. I, for one, consider that with many men their faith has become uninteresting to them because they have not grown out of the imagery into a rational understanding of it. In everything else their mind has become a man's; they have put away the things of a child. In matters of faith alone they are still bound to the language and understanding of their childhood days, with the result that faith has become insipid to their mature minds. Happy are they if their childish imagination does not expose their faith to the attacks of the unsparing rationalism of clever infidelity. It is said of a certain modern English agnostic of a very militant type that the only Christianity he ever knew was the one he learned at the age of five. All his virulence is directed against the childhood Christianity which alone he had known. I will try then to give what I may call a man's account of the doctrine of angelic guardianship; it will be simply the theological view that we find in the writings of our masters.

There are perhaps few things that make a doctrine more insipid to the mature mind than the impression that there is absolute disproportion between means and end, in the would-be spiritual facts embodied in it.

Thus, in the present instance, the idea of one mighty spirit spending his existence in watching over the details of an insignificant human life seems to imply such a disproportion between means and end. One does not send for a giant to pick up straws. Then there is a suspicion that the unceasing presence of a spirit of untiring activity might take away all human responsibility, if the spirit-role is to be taken at all seriously. Why not abandon oneself blindly to a guide in whom power and knowledge are practically unlimited? The Christian who follows up logically his faith in the celestial tutelage need only hope and pray, and leave planning and execution to the spirit who, from his position, is the main partner in the business of life. Such an objection might be formulated with a good deal of plausibility.

When we say that Angels, or at least Guardian Angels, have been created for the benefit of man, we must be understood in the sense which we attach to an analogous expression, that God became Man for the sake of man. In this we do not make man, or mankind, the end for which God became incarnate. Christ the Son of God is infinitely greater than mankind, and the end of His Incarnation could never be man; He Himself is His own *raison d'être*, and He is also the end of man, or mankind. The human individual is redeemed and sanctified precisely with a view to making him worthy of the God incarnate. The fruit of our Redemption is this, that we should be in a fit state to glorify the God incarnate, and have Him for our ultimate end. Otherwise Redemption would not have been a raising up of the *massa humana*. The most effective way in which God could become Man for man's sake was to make Himself, as God-Man, the end of man.

So with the Angels in regard to the children of Adam. If we insist on using the apparently utilitarian expression that Angels were created for us, let us understand it in a way that will be of the fullest advantage to us.

Their protective and guiding action has essentially and exclusively one aim, one purpose: to make us worthy of them, worthy to be one day their fellow-citizens. If they are in any way to be said to have been made for us, it is as the objects of our everlasting contemplation, of our unending joy, in their beauty, of our peace in their company.

Their external, temporary influence on and around us should be considered as a means, they themselves would be the end; their solicitude over us is so vigilant because we are intended to be their companions.

But we need not use the expression that Angels have been made for us. To say that man has been made for the Angels, though less familiar to our ears, would be a great deal truer.

Every human being has been entrusted to the care of an Angel. Christian tradition has it that no two human beings are entrusted to the same spirit. This, of course, must be understood of two persons who are making their earthly pilgrimage at the same time. The reason, for this exclusive guardianship, one man one Angel, could never be any inability in angelic knowledge or power to take care of many at the same time; this would be derogatory to spirit-activity.

The reason must be looked for in the moral relationship which such intimacy and union, as is inherent in the Angel's guardianship, is intended to establish forever between man and his tutelary spirit. This loving appropriation by the spirit of one of the human family does not mean exclusion of any other sort of concurrent activity in other spheres, according to the power and order of the Angel. I do not speak here of that holiest and highest of his activities, to behold without ceasing the Face of the Father who is in heaven. I refer rather to his influence on some other creature. Nor does it mean constant and unceasing presence.

We know what angelic presence implies. A spirit is present because he acts on the material, the human being; if he ceases to act, he is already departed, back in the infinitely distant spirit-world.

On the other hand, the Angel's will, his inward determination to act, has already made him present again. Constancy, permanence of guardianship, according to Saint Thomas, is preserved through this instantaneous approach from the spirit-world, provided the spirit be never without a full knowledge of all that concerns his charge. Saint Thomas does not speak of constant, unceasing action: therefore he does not assume unceasing local presence, as the one follows from the other. All that Saint Thomas requires, to make the guardianship unceasing, is that the Angel should be continually mindful of his ward.

Distance does not exist for spirits.

Three things would thus constitute the office of the Guardian Angel. First, an intimate and complete knowledge of the human person under his care; this knowledge goes beyond what an Angel is enabled to know of created things generally, it embraces a knowledge of the secrets of the heart. In the second place, there is determination in the Angel's will to help, whenever it is necessary or useful. Thirdly, there is the action itself, on or about the person, which constitutes the presence.

The doctrine that no two Angels are of equal rank is not forgotten here. The Guardian Angels do not constitute, as it were, one common family of Angels; they are all spirits belonging to the angelic world, every one more important to the completeness of that world than is any heavenly body in the stellar world. "There is no reason," says the Angelic Doctor, "why an Angel should not have the care of a human being, though he be superior to another Angel, on whom he exerts spiritual influences as on an inferior."

We have said already that to watch over a member of the human family does not by any means exhaust the Angel's activity, even at

one and the same time. Nor would it necessarily mean a preference, a privilege, for a man to be under the care of a higher spirit.
The advantage would consist in the amount of activity of any
given spirit over his charge.

These theological considerations make the doctrine of Guardian Angels one full of dignity, capable of appealing to the most
cautious and exacting mind. But there is another aspect put forward by Saint Thomas, which ought not to be forgotten, and
which safeguards the majesty of this dogma which has been familiar to us from the nursery. In order to give satisfaction to our intellect, which seems to dislike the thought of a celestial prince
being tied to the service of a mortal man, Aquinas repeats with
great insistence that we must distinguish between what is transitory and what is everlasting. The soul is everlasting, while everything else is transitory, however vast and extensive it may be.
Therefore, the human soul is worthy of the attention of a spirit,
even of the highest rank.

I dare say most people, who would sneer at the Catholic tradition
of "one man, one Angel," would find it at least a beautiful idea to
suggest that God had appointed one of the heavenly powers to
watch over the destinies of the British Empire. Yet the British
Empire is something merely temporal; the soul of every single man
is eternal! Catholic spiritism, if we may use this term for Catholic
theology on spirits, far from degenerating into a dabbling with
the Unseen, makes a man more simple in faith, which is of things
that are not seen. Moreover, far from making the spirits the agents
of his pet desires, it makes him realize his own responsibilities.

These thoughts are in their place here, as we consider the
nature of the influence our Guardian Angel exerts over each one
of us. Our masters in sacred doctrine make angelic action begin
only where human resources fail.

We may first mention that part of the Angel's activity that is
outside us, keeping from us any possible dangers, which only a

higher intellect could foresee; or bringing about circumstances that would make for our ultimate happiness, and which it would take a genius more than human to arrange. Of the Angel's opposition to the powers of darkness I speak in another chapter. This too is a field of activity which requires more than flesh and blood.

But I come to the more human part of the question, that part which deals with what is inside us. The Angel finds there, in our mind and in our heart, room enough for activity which he alone can supply.

Three functions may be ascribed to him: to give our thoughts a new train, in speculative things; to help us to decide prudently in particular matters, where decision is required, and where no hard-and-fast rules are available; to alter the disposition of our lower appetites when they are set against our spiritual good.

All these three effects require an outside agent, or anyhow may be produced by an outside agent, without lightening in the least the burden of personal responsibility on the part of man.

Before proceeding, there is one very important consideration deserving of our attention. Saint Thomas makes the Angel's power in the interior life of man dependent on the pre-existing disposition of the senses, external and internal. The Angel cannot act directly on the pure intellect, nor can he touch the will. He must make use of the senses and of previous sensitive acquisitions which he finds in man. It is thus he reaches the intellect. Modern spiritualism, in so far as there is reality in it, will bear out this law of spirit-activity on man. This alone would suffice to safeguard man's liberty, under the action of his angelic protector. The spirit makes use only of what is offered to him by man's moral state.

With regard to external action on the spirit the following threefold gradation has been adopted by our masters. First, God alone is able to touch the intellect and the will directly, whether in Angels or in men. Secondly, a created spirit in a state of pure immateriality is able to touch directly the intellect of another created spirit in the same state of immateriality. Thirdly, an Angel cannot touch directly the intellect not yet in a state of pure immateriality, as is the condition of the human intellect during the present life. He has to approach it through the senses. The reason is obvious: we ourselves receive all our knowledge through the observation of our senses, and our intellectual life is closely linked with our sense-life. Even an Angel has to conform to the laws of the nature with which he is dealing.

It is a universal axiom with all theologians that God alone is able to touch directly, and handle, as it were, a created free will. It is one of the exclusive and incommunicable privileges of the Godhead. Created agencies may persuade, may entice; the Almighty alone can enter into the innermost recesses of created volition and change it.

Saint Thomas gives the reason of this exclusive power of God on created volition. It is perfectly simple, and easy to follow. An act of volition would not be an act of free will if it were not essentially a following of the will's own desire and inclination. It is the will's very nature to follow its own dictates, as its own. Now, when an outside agent is said to change the will, it implies this: the outside agent must make the will follow the new inclinations as coming from itself, i.e., with complete freedom, otherwise it would not be an act of free will. This then supposes that the nature of the will itself has been changed. For it could not follow a new bent as its own unless it had been made such as to have this new bent. Now God alone, who is the Maker of natures, can alter them. Therefore God alone can alter a created will. We must bear in mind, when reading this Scholastic argument, that it is all about the purely spiritual will, where there is freedom of election.

These considerations need not be looked upon as a digression. They belong to the very heart of the matter—angelic influence on man. They help us to map out the field of that influence, either good or evil; for many of the views expressed here hold good for the influence of the evil spirit on man, though, for the present, we speak of good influences only. The remarks made just now make it clear, not only that human responsibility is not superseded by angelic assistance, but also that there is left an immense sphere in man for the direct action of God. In his action the Guardian Angel is respectful both of our own and of God's share in our mental and moral operations.

But to come back now to what are the Angel's proper spheres within us, we said first that he may be the originator of a new train of thoughts that will lead to what is good.

We all know from experience what it is to have our mind put on a new track. We shall find in most cases that the new suggestion comes from something that is not ourselves; it may be human words, oral or written; it may be some external event. Looking back, we feel thankful to the man, or the book, or the circumstance, that made our former thoughts leave their accustomed groove, and started us on a new line altogether.

Thus a businessman may owe his success to a new way of thinking of the things of his trade that came to him casually, it would seem, but certainly from the outside. What I say is this: without excluding such inferior influences, or origins of new trains of thought, according to Catholic theology there is a spirit that has been appointed to be for us a source of new lights. We all have to confess to a constant tendency to direct all our thoughts into one specific channel; it comes from the limitations of our nature. The heavenly spirit who is our partner in the business of life is made just the other way: his views embrace everything at every moment; his is a most elastic mind, not crystallized into any particular shape; he makes us think new thoughts. This fact has a most universal application; it is true of the purely supernatural, as well as of the natural, the temporal.

The Angel of God can give the victorious idea to the general on the battlefield, or make the recluse think of higher things for his own soul's profit. Yet no influence could stand less in the way of human initiative and responsibility than the one just described.

We have mentioned practical decision in everyday life as the second sphere of the Angel's operation. Here, too, the Angel stands in no one's way, and his presence is indispensable, if our life is to be a success in the eyes of God.

Saint Thomas remarks very wisely that even if all virtues had been liberally infused into the soul by God, and had made man perfect, the virtue of prudence would make a higher, an external assistance necessary.

Prudence has to deal with facts about which there are no *a priori*, no universal rules. To know what is best in a given case is, not infrequently guesswork for the holiest, wisest, and most experienced. At such times we want a counselor, and we do not feel that his advice is an intrusion, a curtailing of our freedom or responsibility.

Theology points to the Angel who guards us as the born adviser and counselor of man in affairs that have no other rule than their endless variability.

Finally there are our moods and feelings, our emotions and obstinacies, coming from confirmed antipathies. All these spring from our lower appetites. The will falls an easy prey to them. We do in a passion what we regret when the storm is over.

Here is the most fertile source of our moral falls. The appetites that ought to be under our control are allowed to overpower us. Here too we know what important changes are brought about by things that are outside us; how the wrath of an Achilles vanishes before a fair smile; how the gentle word is as oil on troubled waters.

Nothing ought to convince us so firmly of the humanity of Catholic theology as this fact, that in it the Angel of God appears as the born appeaser of man's rebellious appetites, through psychic influences of an infinitely delicate nature.

Such then is the gift of God to man. Like all divine gifts, it may be hidden forever in a napkin, or it may be made to produce a hundredfold. What we have said of the inaccessibility of free will, together with that necessity under which the angelic spirit lies to make use only of those dispositions which he finds in man, is the explanation of so much failure in results.

To some minds it may seem a grave doctrinal difficulty that, with such powerful spirit-protection over every human individual, so few lives should be a moral success; they may think the theory of angelic guardianship improbable on that score. But one might just as well doubt God's constant presence and action in the human soul; there too the obvious results are not in keeping with what I might call God's lavish expenditure of grace.

But all we want for the universal laws of the moral order, for the generous dispositions of divine Providence, is this: that they are at the command of whomsoever is willing to make use of them. Man is constantly abusing his own beautiful nature, his own glorious faculties, yet that human nature is left to him; any day he chooses he may make it the instrument of sainthood.

So likewise, he may ignore and render ineffectual the angelic partnership; but the day he is resolved to turn it to good account, he will find it to be a mine of hidden moral wealth.

One more practical consideration before concluding this chapter. Does it not seem strange that one should be actually incapable of ever detecting whether a fresh idea, an advice, a good movement, comes from the Angel of God? Yet such is the hard fact. We never claim to know that we have been led to any particular conclusion by an angelic spirit. And yet all the time we have to look up to him as our God-given counselor and guide. In this we have a noticeable instance of the soundness and healthiness of what I might call Catholic spiritualism.

It would be a serious loss to our moral life, in fact it would deprive it of all dignity, if we did not think or decide any more for ourselves, if we had within us, clearly and distinctly, the thought and decision of someone else; it would lower us to the level of mere automatons.

Such is the strength and subtlety of those blessed spirits that they make their own suggestions appear to us as our own thoughts; or rather, they make them to be our own thoughts, our own impressions, for which we shall get the glory, the good renown before God and man.

Among men, a clever counselor will so insinuate his own views into the mind of another whom he advises, as to make that man look on the new thought as coming from the hidden recesses of his own mind. Angelic advice and assistance is of that sort. To know whether the illumination comes from the Angel of God is of secondary importance. The important thing is to be in such a state, morally, as to be fit to receive the angelic influence.

And we know well enough at any time of our life what is necessary to be in that state.

CHAPTER 48

Guardian Angels and Divine Providence

Saint Thomas speaks of the appointing of a heavenly spirit to be the exclusive guardian of a particular human being as the practical application of divine Providence with regard to man.

Providence, or the guiding vigilance of the Creator over His creatures, is part of the order of Nature. God would not be a wise Creator if He left the creature all to its own resources.

Now Saint Thomas implies that Providence is not a direct act of God, but a mediated act. The direct and immediate executive powers of Providence are the celestial spirits; they are Providence in practice, and therefore they become one of the main factors in the world's course. We can never give too great prominence to the Scholastic principle that God Himself never does directly what may be achieved through created causality. It would be quite within the spirit of Catholic theology to say that for any result which does not require actually infinite power, God would sooner create a new spiritual being capable of producing that result, than produce it immediately Himself. Now it is certainly a very remarkable fact that the fall of man, whatever changes it may have brought about in his relationship to the spiritual world, has not interfered in the least with that close association of the individual human being with one of the heavenly powers; and no less remarkable is this, that our masters cannot conceive of any human individual so sunk in evil as to be forsaken forever by his guardian Angel.

Catholic tradition has it that Antichrist, being the man of sin, will be the most criminal of human beings that ever lived; and therefore our masters asked themselves the question, whether even Antichrist will have a guardian Angel; they take this extreme case in order to emphasize the extent of the doctrine. Of course their answer is invariably in favor of an Angel being the guardian even of Antichrist; for even he, says Saint Thomas, owing to the presence of the bright spirit, will do less harm than if he were left to himself.

All this goes to show that we are here face to face with a great moral law of creation, admitting of no exception, universal, unending in its applications and its resourcefulness. It is not the effect of a special providence, a matter of privilege; for whatever was special providence was lost through the fall. It may therefore be safely asserted that man is simply incapable of attaining his spiritual end without the cooperation of his Guardian Angel; that cooperation is as absolute a necessity as are the physical laws that maintain his bodily life.

The doctrine of Guardian Angels is not primarily a devotional stimulus, something given purposely to foster piety and spiritual life, any more than the doctrine of God's constant presence within our being, though, of course, it may be a fruitful source of real devotion. We simply live on it, and live through it, if we live at all; but like other doctrinal facts not primarily devotional, as, for instance, creation, it may become for the individual soul a personal revelation, if that soul gives it its special attention; and it may have for that soul all the reality of meaning which it was at first intended to have for everyone.

This would be the place to consider the Guardian Angel's role with man in the state of innocence; for man even in that happy state of perfect moral and intellectual integrity had his Guardian Angel. According to theology, man's original endowments were not such as to render superfluous the tutelage of a higher spirit. It might be said, of course, that the Angel was to Adam like a friend making happier the state of happiness; but this is not exactly the mission of the guardian spirit, who must be essentially a protector against danger, and who, even in the state of primitive integrity, was a necessary help to man, in a province where man alone would not have been equal to his circumstances. Saint Thomas, with great theological candor, says that the protection was necessary even then against the assaults of the fallen angels.

I dare say there is hardly anything in Catholic theology less popular with the modern mind than the idea of a perfectly innocent creature, as primeval man is supposed to have been, being surrounded by hosts of spiritual enemies, of much more powerful natures than his own. How did they come in? is a question that naturally arises; there seems to be a certain unfairness in such a condition. But unfairness of condition there could not be, through the very fact of there being an Angel given to man to counteract the spirit of darkness. As the state of innocence is the one state God purposely designed for man, all natural and supernatural provisions for the benefit of man are seen in that state in their proper proportion and role; therefore it must be said that whatever new duties the tutelary spirit took on himself for the sake of man through the Fall, the natural, congenial, and I might almost say the adequate work or role of the Guardian Angel is to resist the evil spirit that besets man; for such, and such alone, was his office in Paradise.

This will, of course, lead up to a conclusion which will be rather unexpected for many minds, i.e. that the fallen spirits have, in this world of ours, a naturally impregnable position, and, as it were, a prior reason to be there; for only on that assumption can we understand the necessity of angelic protection. Catholic theology has no difficulty in admitting this priority of occupation of the earth by the fallen spirits; it may be a mystery, but it is not a contradiction of any known laws of right and wrong.

We may mention briefly what may be called the Protestant objection to the doctrine of Guardian Angels. It is a part of Protestant mentality to feel worried and annoyed at what is called "the being that stands between man and God." Why should we depend on the intermediary activities of an Angel, and not receive our gifts straight from God? But this objection, if carried to its logical conclusion, would make Nature itself not only superfluous but burdensome, because many things come to us through the workings of Nature which after all would be in the power of God to distribute direct.

The Protestant mind mistakes exclusiveness for immediateness; it thinks that man is nearer to God if there is nothing else but God. The Catholic view, on the contrary, is that the greatest and highest communication of God is the participation of causality. Not only is He the cause of all things and of all good, but He makes His creatures also to be, in their respective degree, causes of things and causes of good; and in our metaphysics, as well as in our piety, we go by this principle, that the highest creature is also the most powerful creature, and that the more God loves a spiritual being, the more means He gives to that being of doing good to others. In fact a creature without its participated powers of causality, most likely implies contradiction. That goodness is communicative of itself is a far-reaching Scholastic principle, and the more goodness there is in a spiritual being, the more it gives of itself.

Chapter 49

Angelic Knowledge

There is perhaps no phenomenon that strikes a thoughtful mind more forcibly than the absolute disproportion between human knowledge and the number of things that make up the world. The world is immense; wherever we go we find new things, and man knows next to nothing about them; it always is and always will be a sealed book; he may behold the cover of the book and may even count the number of seals, but as to reading it! So evidently the world is much vaster than the human mind, at least in its present state.

Now we may put the problem like this: is it always and everywhere the case, that the things that are, should be greater and more numerous than the things that are known? Will it always be that a vast part of the world is beyond created knowledge, is unfathomable by finite science? Or is it not rather the ordinary state of things, that created knowledge should precede the created things, should be commensurate with those things and, if anything, should be superior to them, so that the knowing of the things should be in a way more important than their actual existence? The generic term "thing" used here stands for every sort of being that is not a spiritual entity, and which therefore has no knowledge of its own existence.

It would hardly be a satisfactory solution to say that God knows the things He created and that therefore knowledge ranks prior to existence. The knowledge God has of the work of His own hands could be no satisfactory reason for the existence of so much that is not known by us. For it is a case of created knowledge versus the created unknown.

Catholic theology has boldly taken up the attitude expressed in the second alternative, that knowledge is prior to, and more important than, the existence of the thing; that whatever receives existence at the hands of God is made first an object of a new contemplation to a created mind. The normal state then is this, more knowledge than existing things; the opposite is an exceptional state. Saint Thomas lays down this proposition: whatever God does, in the natural order of things, He first makes it known to the created immaterial spirit. This may be considered as the Scholastic principle of angelic cognition.

We may adopt this principle with perfect confidence. It may at first sight look unphilosophic, unworthy of great metaphysicians. Man has to find the few treasures of Nature, which he is able to discover, by the sweat of his brow; he that adds to science, adds to labor, and an *a priori* possession of all knowledge, as a natural gift, inborn, without any labor, might seem to be a kind of spiritual or intellectual fairy-tale. Yet we might as well be surprised to see the world exist without any laborious process of its own, as to hear that there are minds made in such a wise as to have a perfect and full cognizance of everything that is. With our masters then, let us simply accept the following theory: a spirit comes into existence with the knowledge of all material, created things, and their laws and the results of the laws, *ad infinitum*. There is no less difficulty in admitting the existence of such a complex universe as we see, than in admitting perfect knowledge of it in a created mind. Both come equally from the hands of God. Besides this, every spirit is born with a clear knowledge of every other spirit in things that are not free will; but the lower spirit is not capable of understanding the higher spirit with the same vividness with which the higher spirit understands his own nature.

The propositions here laid down admit of no exception. Whatever God does to build up the universe, He first produces the idea and image of it in the angelic mind. Even a lost spirit is not deprived of this action of God on the created intellect. It is not grace, it is nature, and nature has not been diminished in the lost spirit.

This is what our masters mean to express by saying that spirits receive their knowledge, not from the thing that is, but direct from God. We need not enter here into a controversy as to whether the knowledge of all these things is an attribute of their nature, or whether God, by a direct act, fills their intellect with science. All we need grasp here is that absolute "a-prioriness" of angelic cognition.

There is one vast section of things however that has a unique character and presents an exceptionally difficult problem to our minds in this matter of both divine and angelic knowledge, I mean the acts of the free will in the spirit and in man. They are free, because they are not necessarily pre-contained in any cause. If they were pre-contained, they would be no longer free.

Any natural phenomenon that happens, say in the center of the earth, is infallibly pre-contained in some laws, in some elements; and the knowledge of those laws and elements would enable a mind to foresee its happening. My free act is not so pre-contained in any law or element, even spiritual. That God knows such acts is a matter of faith; we even feel instinctively that He knows them.

How He knows them, or, as theologians say, what is His medium of knowing them, as they are not His own free acts, is the debatable question that has divided theologians into two great camps, commonly called Thomists and Molonists.

What we have to remember here is that no created nature, however perfect, could be made such as to be the medium of knowing one single act of free will of another free creature. Whatever is a free act in the creature, or the result of a free act, even an Angel knows only as far as God reveals it to him. As to the extent of that revelation to any particular spirit, we have no certain data to go by. Everything would point to a liberal manifestation on the part of God of acts of free will, either present or future.

There is no contradiction in this idea of a spirit, though he be but a finite and created being, having, through the operation of God, knowledge of an immense number of created things, or acts of the created free will. (It is a matter of theological certainty that the human soul of Our Lord had such a knowledge of an infinitely long series of free acts, as He knows all the deeds and thoughts of all creatures, angelic and human, in the past, present and future.)

The universal rule for what might be called the amount of knowledge of these free acts is laid down by Saint Thomas; whatever belongs in any way to any spirit, and has any relation to him, is made known to him through the act of God. God is as present in the spiritual intellect, and as constantly at work there, as He is in the innermost part of every creature, where He works incessantly to keep it in existence. There seems in fact to be a close relation between God's action in the angelic intellect and God's action in every creature, called conservation, and which is creation continued; one follows from the other, and they both are of the natural order of things.

Here we may speak of a subject on which our masters in theology have written much; a most abstruse and difficult subject it is, and they all declare it to be one of the hardest problems in divinity. It is a problem too, which, unless handled by a master mind, might easily become an object of ridicule. It is *locutio angelica*, the speech of the Angel. How do Angels or spirits generally communicate? That they do communicate is proved by Scripture; not to mention the fact that it is precisely what we should expect spirits to do. They could not form a hierarchic society, without speech or communication of some kind. What method have they of transmitting their thoughts into the mind of another spirit? If we remember all that has been said about the nature of a spirit and about the "a-prioriness" of all his knowledge, these questions will become the more perplexing, the more we ponder them.

The answer of Saint Thomas, however, is very simple and worthy of the high subject. The process comes to this: a spirit intends effectually to communicate his own thought to another spirit; from the very fact of that intention and direction the thought of the speaking spirit belongs to what might be called the sphere of the spirit thus addressed; and the spirit thus addressed knows it, as he knows every free act that has any relation to him. We cannot go beyond this very simple theory of Saint Thomas. Needless to repeat here that there is no such thing as distance for spirits; and even if there were distance, it would be no obstacle to direct and immediate communication of thought.

All this, of course, is true also of the human spirit in the state of separation from the body; and also in the state of the reunion with the body, as in the resurrection the soul animates the body not as soul, but as spirit.

CHAPTER 50

Angelic Illumination

There is a book, written in the early centuries of the Christian era, which has left a deep mark on Catholic theology. It is the *Celestial Hierarchy* of Denis the Areopagite. The Schoolmen gave Saint Denis the Athenian, a convert of Saint Paul, the credit of its authorship. Modern research is against this ascription; it considers that the book was written about the fifth century by a Greek monk. We need not take sides in this controversy, as the influence of the writing is to be attributed not so much to the author as to the book itself.

As with the *Imitation of Christ*, the author is nowhere. It is its theology that has gained for it such an important place in the development of Christian doctrine. Few works of the past are quoted so frequently by the Schoolmen. It is certainly a most original book and its views truly deserve to be called, as the mediaeval mystics used to call them, heavenly. All its doctrines have passed into Catholic theology, and Saint Thomas brought his own genius to bear on it, and made it part of his wonderful dogmatic structure. It is there that he found all his teaching concerning angelic *illuminatio*, which holds such an important place in his doctrine on the Angels, and also on the human soul.

The main theme of the old Greek book is this, that the great specific differentiations between the celestial spirits, far from creating distance and separation, are the origin of wonderful communications and spirit-interchanges which make of the spirit-world one harmonious organism. As diversity of rank, from Scripture and Tradition, is evidently the first feature that strikes the theologian, the Celestial Hierarchy gives what might be called the connecting link between all the spirit-ranks. Without this communion, the spirit-world could not be considered to be one great universe. It would be a mere aggregate, of mighty beings indeed, but all isolated. The connecting link is the angelic illumination.

The idea is this: the highest spirit is through the very height of his nature endowed with vastly more knowledge than the lower spirit. Now the higher spirit gives of his superabundance to the lower spirit, and through that influence of his makes the lower spirit the participant of his own excellencies, and thus lifts him above his own nature, so that a spirit benefits in some degree by the excellencies of all the spirits that are above him.

It is thus that created causality, which is the highest gift of the Creator to the creature, finds scope in the spirit-world. The objection that comes so frequently to the mind: why does not God do the thing Himself? may be considered here more particularly. Its refutation will be a great gain to our mind.

We suppose here with all theologians that God is as fully and as completely near any spirit of any rank as the nature of the spirit allows. We suppose that God's action is exerted to its full extent, so that nothing of God's action is withheld. Thirdly, we suppose that everything in the creature that possibly could go out to God, has gone out to Him. Now when all these conditions are fulfilled, we maintain that there is still something in the created spirit, human or angelic, that may be improved, if such an expression be permissible. Catholic feeling about the benefit derived from the influence of God's elect on fellow-creatures in no wise proceeds from a feeling that God does something but not everything; that He leaves half of the work to the created spiritual agency. No, this is not Catholic doctrine, it is the reverse. When God's action has been in contact with every possible point of our being, we still feel that there is a created influence that can bring us nearer to God.

So in this matter of angelic illumination; no intercourse could be more close and direct than that between a celestial spirit and

God; in all that which is, in any way, a point of contact for God in that spirit, God is there Himself, without any intermediary. The spirit, on his part, responds to God's approaches wholeheartedly, unreservedly. Yet even after that, according to theology, there is still room for what I have called improvement, through the very fact of the spirit being a separate personality from God, of his being a created, not a divine nature. A spirit has with a fellow-spirit points of contact and relationships which have exclusively the created for their object, not the Uncreated.

This then is the office and mission of *illuminatio angelica*, that whatever in a spirit is a point of contact for a fellow-spirit, the higher spirit should make use of, should work on it, and through his pure influence should raise it up to God.

This explanation of that duality of relationship, one with God and one with the creature, is a most important thing in every branch of theology, and finds its highest as well as its most necessary application in the state of the eternal and supernatural happiness for Angels and for man, where the Vision of God, though full happiness, is not all happiness.

It is through the imparting of knowledge that the Angels of God make the human soul happy, with an additional happiness, and thus they treat it as a brother-spirit.

CHAPTER 51

The Number of Angels

It is an article of faith that the number of Angels created by God is exceedingly great. There has been no official pronouncement of Pope or universal Council on the subject, it is true. But the doctrine has always been so popular, so commonly received, that the official pronouncement was never wanted to make it an article of faith. Angels are innumerable; no man on this earth could count them off one by one and get to the end.

In fact, the number of angelic spirits has always been considered as one of the marvels of God's power that baffle the human mind. We know, of course, that it could not be infinite; an actually infinite series of beings seems to involve metaphysical contradiction. There is one Angel who is first, and there is another Angel who is last. But a successive counting of them will not reach the last one; those that see them all, have to see them simultaneously.

All this we may grant easily. Nature, such as it is before our eyes, has habituated us to the numberless. It is an indispensable notion in science. Yet, in this case, a difficulty of a metaphysical order arises which makes the angelic innumerability something quite new, something unique, something to set the mind aghast, even with one to whom natural, physical numberlessness is a familiar notion.

The numberless of Nature are invariably beings of the same species, powers or elements of the same kind, and mostly of the class that might be called the infinitely small. They become irresistible powers precisely through their numberlessness.

Not so with the Angels. Every one of them is a being perfect in beauty, power and wisdom. Every one of them belongs to a spiritual sphere or plane of his own, not shared by any other spirit.

Nature's microscopic creatures borrow strength from immense accumulation. Their multiplicity alone makes them into a power. But with the Angels every one is a great power. Therefore, we have to find an explanation for angelic multitude which will differ radically from the explanations we have for physical innumerability, though the second may familiarize us with, and prepare us for the first.

Why then are Angels so numerous, when we know that every one of them is a vaster thing in the spiritual order than the one preceding him?

The end God has in view, in His creative act, is to manifest Himself. This He does in giving existence to numberless spiritual beings, all differing in their attributes.

As we have already said, the material, bodily creation is not the image of God; the spirit alone is God's image, in truth and reality. With material things, multiplication of beings is, I might say, of a utilitarian, provisional character, to bring about certain great physical results, few in number, that are to minister, ultimately, to the spirit. But it would be preposterous to say that God has multiplied the grains of sand on the seashore in order that the many might express some beauty of His which one grain could not express.

There would be little gained, as regards the external representation of God's internal perfection, by multiplying beings of absolutely the same kind and species. Number in that case is only useful, not beautiful. Besides, as already noticed, the very fact of their materiality prevents them from being the image of God.

If therefore creation means manifestation of God's hidden glories, Angels must all differ, and Angels must be all but infinite in number.

They must be spirits, because spirits alone are truly the image or representation of God. They must differ, so that one may mirror that aspect of divine beauty which another Angel, through the fact of his finiteness, finds it impossible to do. They must be all but infinite in number, if divine majesty is to be adequately manifested in creation. God's perfections are infinite in number and variety.

Why then should we be scandalized if we hear it said that the Angels differ as so many worlds, and yet are more numerous than the grains of sand on the seashore? Which is the more important work: to make a home for the ocean, or to represent adequately, in a created way, the glory of the Trinity?

One of the first facts that is borne in upon us when we read the

Scriptures and the writings of the Fathers of the Church is the distinction of Angels into various categories or choirs. It is commonly said that there are nine choirs of Angels, because there are only nine mentioned in the Scriptures. This enumeration is not to be found in any particular place, but the names of those choirs are gleaned from all over the sacred books. The gradation adopted by Saint Gregory the Great has certainly strong theological value, and it would be rash, to say the least, to maintain that those various appellations do not indicate various classes of spirits, or that there is no gradation expressed by them.

Saint Thomas, who writes long articles on hierarchical distinctions, and gives the *raison d'être* of the angelic orders, could not forget that according to his theology there are no two Angels of equal spirit-rank and that the second Angel is as superior to the first or lowest as that first is superior to the human soul. The following is his view concerning the traditional angelic hierarchy: every Angel is in himself a full and complete angelic order, much more than any star in the material universe is a center of its own system. Only it is impossible for us, who are so remote from spirit-beings, to understand the cosmic role of a spirit, however important. So we have to be satisfied with much vaguer classifications which take in a wide range of spirits, just as astronomy has to be content with comprehensive classifications that divide the universe into planets, fixed stars, comets and nebulae, and so on, as science is not advanced enough to define the function of every heavenly body.

The angelic differentiations are comprehensive and simple enough. They express, according to our masters, a threefold function: that of giving light, which is the highest function; that of receiving light and giving it again, which is the second or intermediary function; and that of receiving it, without giving it to another angelic spirit.

Chapter 52

Angelic Sin

The theology of the fall of Angels is far from being a merely academic discussion, a kind of metaphysical luxury for the learned; on the contrary it is a necessary doctrine, if our faith is to be able to give an account of itself. The existence and activities of evil spirits are a practical question, with practical results, both in ascetical and liturgical life. It is therefore important for us to know how Angels came to be evil spirits. It has, of course, always been a temptation for the human mind to picture to itself a duality of principles, the good and the evil, equally eternal and equally independent, waging war against each other with equal might and skill.

Man's inherent thirst for justice has in most cases preserved him from making the evil principle the final victor. Almost universally, the protagonist of virtue, through some unexpected feat of luck or bravery, is made to gain the mastery; and therein lies the drama of every existence.

Nothing could be more abhorrent to the Catholic mind than a duality of principles. Whatever might be said to the contrary, the Christian tradition, if it had any unsound tendency, would tend towards the complete abolition of any doctrine concerning evil spirits, rather than towards the admission of an evil principle such as that just described. Our masters have therefore labored hard to show how spirits could become wicked, though they be still full of God's beauty, and their labors have not been in vain. Their doctrine concerning the sin of the Angels is a masterpiece of intellectual shrewdness and moderation.

It is sin, and sin alone, that makes Satan and his wicked followers differ from Michael and the holy Angels. As Saint Thomas points out, a spirit, without that terrible element of personal sin, could never be, by any manner of means, even an indirect cause of suffering to another. Among mankind the best and holiest may be, without any guilt, a cause or occasion of suffering to someone else.

On the lower levels of nature, the life of one being is often the death of another. The wolf preys on the lamb, though the wolf be no intrinsically evil being; he is an evil being only to his victim.

With entirely spiritual beings, from the very fact of all their activities being in a spiritual sphere, there does not exist even that indirect causation of evil or suffering. A spirit through his nature is totally good, in a twofold sense: all that he is in himself is perfect, and all that he does outside himself invariably produces happiness. The wicked intentions, therefore, with which the evil spirits are credited by Catholic theology, are due entirely to a deliberate act, for which there was no special propensity in the angelic nature; their first sin.

What then is angelic sin? Theologians of all men find it most difficult to believe in evil spirits, because the knowledge they possess of the spirit-nature does not easily associate sin and angelic nature in one being. Most men, no doubt, once they have got themselves to believe in spirits at all, would find it as easy to believe in bad spirits as they believe in bad men. Contrary to what is sometimes said, popular imagination is ready enough to believe in the sin of spirits, because it conceives spirits to be merely a higher kind of changeable beings, like ourselves.

Theology starts with the assumption that spirits are impeccable. But as Revelation declares spirit-sin to be a hard fact, theologians are at pains to find how it could possibly come about. "How is it possible," they ask, "for such mighty beings to fall?" Nothing in their nature seemed to prepare them for that fall, unless it were the fact of their being finite creatures. In their intellect there can be no error: in their will there can be no passion; their only craving and desire could be for spiritual, intellectual riches; but it is invariably a good and praiseworthy thing to desire and crave for spiritual riches.

It has thus become one of the hardest problems of theology to explain the sin of Angels, and to find in it, as an article of faith, grounds for peace and rest. As a fundamental principle, in which Saint Thomas believes firmly, we may lay down this axiom: a spiritual being like an Angel could never err, intellectually or through his will, if left to his merely natural state. A spirit, as spirit, is simply impeccable. True, his will is free, but his nature is so perfect as to exclude even the remotest abuse of freedom. In the natural state he only need follow the prompting of his nature to be pure; and the more he follows those natural inclinations, the purer he is. Therefore he is a rule unto himself, and whatever he does must be infallibly good. But in the supposition of the spirit being raised to a higher state, the supernatural state, both his intellect and his will, as Saint Thomas says, are no longer a rule to themselves. In supernatural things his mind and his will have to submit to a higher rule, the law of God, and there is the possibility of turning away. It is, accordingly, in the elevation of the Angel above his natural state that our master of sacred theology finds the Angel's vulnerability; a clear proof that angelic sin is against the genius of Catholic theology. The objection rises immediately to one's mind: why then did God raise His Angels to the supernatural state? I shall say a word or two presently about this.

A dogma of this kind, representing the brightest of spirits falling from such a sublime height, was bound to give rise to what might be called theological romance, with now and then a tinge of scandal. Byron had his predecessors in certain heretics of the first centuries who thought they had found the key to the fall of the Angels in Genesis 6:4. Where the scandalmongers have been silent, the poet has made of Lucifer a hero of rebellion.

It may be said of theology that it abominates both romance and tragedy. It keeps its discussions on a high speculative level, so high indeed that only a trained theologian is able to follow them. I will attempt, however, to sum up the Catholic tradition in a brief and simple way.

We must bear in mind that great fact which plays such an important role in the theology of Saint Thomas, that every Angel is a separate species, being, as it were, a world to himself, a star in the angelic world, holding in the universe a place of unique importance, in fact, being indispensable to its completeness. If he were not just where he is, the world would not be complete; there would be a gap.

This gives the Angel a wonderful singularity of position. There is something incommunicable in it; it makes his greatness and his beauty; and all this he possesses by nature. To love this position of his, to delight in it, to be ever happy in it, and the thought of its singularity, is not only lawful to him, but it is his very life.

On the other hand, the supernatural, the grace of God, or sanctifying grace, has this characteristic: it is common to all; it is specifically the same in all, and what is more, it may be possessed by beings far inferior to the Angels, such as man. Specifically the same in all, it may be possessed in various degrees which depend on the dispensation of God, and not on the excellencies of the nature that receives it.

This then was Lucifer's fall: rather than be one of many, through the higher but commoner gift of sanctifying grace, he preferred to remain in the singularity of his position and to occupy his unique place as spirit in the natural universe.

Thus the spirit willfully and deliberately placed himself in opposition to the order of God. It is God's express and unchanging will that every spiritual creature should be raised to the supernatural state, and the spiritual world as a whole not only strives after the supernatural state with all its might, but the supernatural is the principal part of its life, and the natural is only the secondary function. Therefore the spirit that refuses the supernatural is, through his own choice, in opposition both to the will of God and to the harmony of the spiritual world. He is essentially an outcast, a lost spirit, radically and fundamentally in opposition to eternal life, which is the grace of God; and herein lies the greatness of his fall.

It must be borne in mind that his spirit-position in the universe is the same as before. He could not be replaced unless God annihilated him, and created a new spirit. It might be said that Lucifer and his angels got what they wanted, what their intellect had judged to be their best way of being singular. With them the loss of a higher good could never be matter of regret, as the very absence of that higher good is the condition of their singularity. That they should possess such singularity with the addition of spiritual sufferings, which are the result of their being deliberately in opposition to the harmony of the universe, does not make them either capable of, or anxious for, change, as those sufferings are the direct result of their confirmed determination not to change. As Saint Thomas points out so clearly, the fallen spirits have lost none of their intellectual privileges; there is not the slightest obscurity in their mind. Their will, too, is as passionless, as remote from things unspiritual, as before; the only thing they hate is the grace of God, the supernatural; and if through their suggestion man is tempted to the lowest acts of sensuality, it is not from a love of sin they tempt him, but with a view to preventing him from possessing the grace of God.

It has become clear, I hope, how the first sin of the spirit was pride, and could be nothing else than pride. We apply the word "pride" to many of our transgressions; but pride, properly so called, and as distinct from every other sin, is the love of one's own excellency in opposition to somebody else's, because that other excellency would end the singularity of our own.

The great refusal of the supernatural life made by Lucifer came from his unwillingness to share it with other beings; that would have meant the loss of his singularity. It is sin such as man has never known; this one sin exceeds in guilt millions of sins committed by man. The energetic and terrible metaphors employed in the sacred Scripture concerning the fall of Lucifer become more comprehensible through those very reserves in our theology which I have mentioned. If Our Lord says that He saw Satan fall from heaven like lightning, it is not stronger than the contention of theology when it maintains that Satan put himself into a state of opposition to the grace of God.

The preceding explanations are the best commentary on the frequently used expression that Lucifer coveted to be like unto God. With Saint Thomas I say that it would have been absolutely impossible for Satan to have a desire to be God, or to be equal to God, or to have any of the divine attributes. Such a pretension on the part of an Angel is clearly an impossible one. But to remain in the singularity of his natural position was an imitation of God's position, who is unique, besides being one.

Jealousy is one of the sins most frequently associated with the fall of the Angels. We must of course exclude the idea of jealousy as found in man, with whom it is one of the meaner passions. Jealousy with Satan could only mean spiritual sorrow and opposition at seeing beings lower than himself, such as man, exalted above himself, through the grace of God. Jealousy therefore could not be the first sin, but could only be the consequence of pride.

There has been a good deal of controversy as to whether the mystery of the Incarnation, manifested to the Angels in the light of God, entered to a certain extent into their fall. This may be readily granted, as it tallies fully with all we have said; for it is chiefly in the mystery of the Incarnation that Lucifer was expected to enter into communion with beings lower than himself.

What I have been at pains to do here is to show the wisdom and moderation of our theology. One word more to redeem my promise, and to explain why it was better for God to raise angelic Nature to the supernatural state, though this elevation made the spirit vulnerable and peccable.

God did not set a snare for the fidelity of the Angels, but through an act of His omnipotence He raised created beauty above itself. Now it would be against God's wisdom and kindness to withhold from the world of His beloved spirits the great additional glory of the supernatural state, simply because a minority among them, through their own act, would find in this elevation their ruin. Saint Thomas states expressly that the majority of the Angels remained faithful; nay, he seems to consider that the fallen angels are exceptional cases; he gives this deep reason, that things that are against nature happen but rarely. Now though to be raised to the supernatural is above the angelic nature, to rebel against that elevation is against the promptings of the angelic nature. Why should God pass by the host of faithful spirits and deprive them of the highest happiness because His act of liberality would be an occasion of ruin for a rebellious company?

Before concluding this chapter I may be allowed to make a few remarks with no particular link between them, except that they will help to elucidate several points which have been touched upon already. The incorruptibility of mind of the fallen angels is absolute, and to such an extent is this true, according to Saint Thomas, that neither God nor the good Angels have ceased to communicate to them those lights which belong to the angelic nature. God still enlightens their intellects in all matters that belong to the natural state of the spirit. The only things about which they are kept in ignorance are the mysteries of divine grace. Those mysteries are communicated to the good Angels; their brightness is such that the bad spirits may be said to be in darkness.

When we speak of the pride of rebellious spirits we do not mean, and cannot mean, an evil habit, an unruly propensity which they had from the beginning and which proved their temptation; nothing of the kind could be in an Angel, as he comes direct from the hand of God. Angelic sin was entirely an *act*; the act itself was the pride. The Angel preferred his singularity with the loss of divine grace; and this choice was his pride. We must represent to ourselves the Angel, the moment before the fall, in what I might call a state of perfect equilibrium in mind and will, with no bias one way or the other; or if there was bias, it was towards accepting divine grace, as he had sufficient actual grace to bring about that acceptance. One might say that no act was ever more deliberate, and more impartially calculated.

When we say here that some of the spirits refused sanctifying grace, we do not mean that they had sanctifying grace offered to them, and rejected it; it is an article of faith that they were created in grace, so that they never existed without it. Saint Thomas says that they actually worked with it and merited the Beatific Vision through it; but they fell out of it, so to speak, which of course makes their opposition to it all the more radical, and their rebellion all the more formidable, as they had already tasted its sweetness. This is why they may be called apostate spirits, since they fell away from the supernatural state. We must remember that the grace they were granted in their creation was ineffably great, and God alone knows what treasures of supernatural beauty enriched their minds. The heaven which preceded the fall of the angels could never mean, of course, the heaven of the Blessed where God is seen face to face, for there is no falling away from the vision of God. It was a lower kind of heaven from which they fell.

When we speak of the "hideousness" of the fallen spirits the term must of course be understood of their perverted will; it is, to put it quite theologically, their constant, unceasing effort to destroy the grace of God, wherever it is to be found.

Conclusion

In the last chapters of this modest treatise I have taken the reader up to the highest summits of Catholic theology—angelic life.

There is a great craving for spirituality in the hearts of many people; spirituality means vitality and endless activity to them. The human soul is destined to be the natural companion of the spirits that dwell with God; angelic illumination is simply another word for vitality and spiritual activity going on forever.

There is nothing deeper, nothing kinder, nothing more merciful, than the Catholic theology of the human soul. It combines the oldest and most persevering sentiments with the highest and most exact thought. Even an unbeliever would do well to study it for its sheer power, harmony and depth; just as an atheist may travel thousands of miles to see the splendors of Saint Peter's in Rome.

But you, dear reader, who have had patience to follow me to the end; whosoever you are, I must remind you once more that, to say the least, the odds are a thousand to one that there is in you something marvelously great, something which you cannot understand, something that is at the bottom of all your pure and noble inspirations, something that is the home of conscience and duty: it is your soul.

May it be your life's task to save that soul of yours, because the loss of it could not but be great, as the soul is so great.

RALPH McINERNY (1929–2010) taught at the University of Notre Dame for over five decades, as both a Professor of Philosophy and the Michael P. Grace Professor of Medieval Studies. He was a prolific author of over two dozen scholarly books, in addition to more than 80 novels, most famously the Father Dowling mystery series. One of the most important Catholic philosophers of his generation, he was a renowned expert on the works of Aristotle and Aquinas. His books include *The Very Rich Hours of Jacques Maritain: A Spiritual Life* and *I Alone Have Escaped to Tell You*, his autobiography.

Zaccheus Press

Zaccheus Press is a small Catholic press devoted to publishing fine books for all readers seeking a deeper understanding of the Catholic faith.

To learn more about Zaccheus Press, please visit our webpage. We welcome your comments, questions, and suggestions.

www.zaccheuspress.com

And behold, there was a rich man named Zaccheus, who was the chief among the tax collectors. And he sought to see Jesus, but could not because of the crowd, for he was short of stature. So he ran ahead and climbed up into a sycamore tree to see Him, for He was going to pass that way.

–Luke 19:2-4